What Can I Say?

How to Talk to People in Grief

What Can I Say?

How to Talk to People in Grief

by Roger F. Miller

1701 CBP Press
St. Louis, Missouri

Second printing, 1987

CBP Press
Box 179
St. Louis, MO 63166

Library of Congress Cataloging-in-Publication Data
Miller, Roger F., 1950-
    What can I say.

    1. Grief.   2. Death—Psychological aspects.
3. Interpersonal communication.   I. Title
BF575.G7M54   1987   155.9'37   86-26868
ISBN 0-8272-4220-4

Printed in the United States of America

Contents

Dedication

**This book is dedicated with
all love and respect to:**

Rev. Robert Karl Miller
28 August 1925 — 29 March 1981

Even in death, he helped me grow personally and professionally. Dad, if I turn out to be half of the man and a fourth of the minister you were, I'll be doing all right.

I love you.

Acknowledgments

Many persons helped me write this book. I am especially indebted to my brother-in-law, Paul Turner, for giving me the original inspiration to write all this down; my friends, family colleagues and associates who read the outline and manuscripts and provided invaluable encouragement and suggestions. Some of these people are Suzanne Turner, Rev. Jim Harmon, Alan and Freeda Romine, Tom and Beth Dorste, Edie Rhodes, my sister Karla, Jean Bott, Ruth Lepke, funeral directors and friends Ted Gibson, Mark Rossow and Chuck Hastings, Rev. Glen Rosborough and the Rev. Brian McNamara.

My thanks also to all those who contributed their personal experiences to this book for illustrative purposes and clarification, and to Molly Betterton, world-class secretary who assisted with manuscript preparation.

I also appreciate the generosity of my friends Andy and Kathy Kretzinger, proprietors of Kretz Press in Jefferson, for their generosity in the loan of a great electronic typewriter used in the final preparation of this manuscript. I was going to have Molly, the church secretary, type this, but the typewriter was too much fun!

Thanks to my church families in Falls City, Nebraska, and Jefferson, Iowa, who gave ministry to me during the illness and its aftermath; our friends who lent support and encouragement during that same time are also thought of with much affection and gratitude.

Thanks to James Merrell, editor of *The Disciple* magazine, for his permission to use the article "Please Understand" and for his encouragement of my writing efforts over the years.

Thanks to my editor and friend at CBP Press, Herbert H. Lambert, who believed in this book with me. He gave good support and encouragement as we moved along in the process of preparation. Herb also gave me gentle nudges from time to time and kept me working. I know he is a gentleman because of those nudges. What I really deserved was a sharp poke!

Hollie Harbaugh and I coauthored *When My Grandma Died* in 1984. At that time, this book was only half finished, and I put the manuscript on hold indefinitely. I had serious thoughts about abandoning the project. Hollie urged me to complete it and to send it on to the publisher. I really appreciate this.

My thanks also to Dr. Earl Grollman, rabbi of the Beth El Temple Center in Belmont, Massachusetts. Despite his eminence in the field of grief education, he has the ability to make one feel instantly at ease. I appreciate what he has taught me through his books and lectures. I also cherish the moral support he gave me while I was writing this book. His friendship is one of the blessings of my life.

My mother, Sue Miller, was the rock on which we were anchored during Dad's illness. She also helped me immensely during the grief work that followed. I was so happy to find out that she took time out from attending to all of us in order to recover from her own grief. She authored the article "Please Understand," which comprises that afterword of this book. Mom, I love you—and thanks.

Finally, to my own family: my wife, daughter and son: What can I say? I love you with all my heart; how lucky I am to have you as my family.

8

Preface

Someone once said, "Writing is easy; all you have to do is sit down at the typewriter, put in a piece of paper and open up one of your veins."

That was a description with which I could readily identify as I wrote this book. Most of these words came directly from my own spiritual pain and emotional blood.

I wrote it from two points of view. The first is that of the minister, the care-giver, the helping professional who has found some ways to make grief-work easier and more effective for the lay-person. The second point of view is that of a grieving son who has written down feelings and impressions in order to try to make some sense of them. As you will see, the book was born through the pain I experienced at the death of my father, the Rev. Robert Karl Miller. Dad died after being ill for six months with cancer of the lung. During the time that he and the rest of my family lived with this terminal illness, I experienced firsthand what was helpful and what was not helpful in speaking to people in grief. It was just a few weeks after his death that the idea for this book came to me after a conversation with my brother-in-law. Once the outline was finished, I became very anxious to begin the first draft. However, I was working on two other book projects at the time, as well as working full-time at my pastoral position. Two or three false starts were made; the book just wouldn't happen.

I told some people I knew about this project and showed them the outline. Their excitement and eagerness to see the final manuscript convinced me that the subject I address here is one that maintains a presence in the back of everyone's mind. A universal question ministers must answer is, "What do you say to the family of someone who has died?"

Dad died in 1981. Five years later, the book is finally done. In addition to the distractions of full-time job and other writing projects mentioned above, I think I also must have needed some time to sort out the feelings, impressions and events surrounding Dad's illness and death.

Though it sounds like a cliché, it is true that time heals all wounds. I have made a good recovery from my grief over losing Dad. Still, there have been times during the writing of this book when all of the pain, fear and anger came washing back over me, and I felt as if I were right there at Dad's bedside all over again. You may detect anger in some parts of the early chapters of this book. That is because I felt anger when I wrote the first draft, and although the anger has subsided some with the passage of time, some of that anger remains as a part of me. And I think that's okay. Anger, as we shall see, is a definite part of the grief process. It can be used creatively as a stimulus for learning what not to do next time.

To be sure, nothing is ever the same once someone you love dies. While you may rebuild a new life on the foundations of your grief, there is a part of you that will always miss the loved one who is gone. However, as badly as grief hurts, there are good things which can come out of the grief experience. One is a genuine feeling for how other people feel when they grieve, and a willingness to give good grief care with some measure of confidence. This book, and the opportunity to help others in care-giving situations, I count among the good things that came out of my grief experience.

Please understand that what you are about to read is a record of guidelines that I found gave substance to the training I acquired as a pastor and grief-therapist. It is substance that anyone can possess, regardless of credentials. Maybe you can gain an idea or two from reading this book. Maybe you can lay claim to your own inner resources in a care-giving situation.

I hope so.

Roger F. Miller, M. Div.
Jefferson, Iowa

Introduction

Earl Grollman has become internationally recognized as an authority on grief and death. One of his major theses, both in his writing and in his speaking, is that in American society "dead" is still a four-letter word. In this society that is so tolerant of frank, open discussion about almost every other personal subject, talk of death still makes people uncomfortable. They are insecure and anxious to change the topic of conversation to almost anything else. We speak of death—whenever we absolutely must—in hushed tones as our minds race to find a more comfortable subject about which to converse. Conversation about death still offends our sensibilities.

Why is this so? I believe there are two reasons. First, our attitudes about death and grief have come a long way from those of our ancestors. Not so long ago, death was regarded as just another step in the process of life: People were born, grew up, had children, and then died. This was how it was. Medicine was not nearly as advanced as today. While it hurt to lose loved ones, people accepted it when it happened and continued living. Two graphic examples of this are found in my file of "Family History."

My father's father emigrated to this country from southern Sweden about the turn of the century. Grandpa was a little boy at the time, traveling with his family as they sought their fortune in this magic land of opportunity. America had been described in glowing terms by my great-great-uncle Magnus Lund, who had come to America some years before. Uncle Magnus had set up shop in Porter, Indiana, on the southern shore of Lake Michigan. (There's a family story that Magnus saw Lake Michigan and thought it was the Pacific Ocean. He decided to put down his roots because he couldn't go any farther west.) Compared to the standard of living in Sweden at the time, Magnus did prosper beyond his wildest dreams. He sent letters back to the rest of the family in Sweden, urging them to come over and make their fortunes as well. Since the cost of the trip was high, only a part of the family could come at one time.

Once my grandfather's family members were settled into their Indiana home, they developed a brisk correspondence with the relatives back in Sweden. One surviving piece of mail is especially interesting. Both the envelope and the writing paper are bordered in heavy black. This was the customary way to convey bad news. The letter begins with the standard southern Swedish salutation, "Live well!" It then announces the death of one of the infants because of milk fever. Immediately after that announcement, the letter goes into an account of the weather. The tone of the letter conveys an attitude of matter-of-factness about the loss of the child.

My grandfather spent much of his time keeping a diary. As I read over the pages for 1916, I was surprised to find an account of the illness and death of Gramp's brother Ludwig. Grandpa doesn't say what the illness was, but apparently it took over a week to do its grim work. The entry for September 4, 1916, is only two words long: "Ludwig died." According to the rest of the diary, it was back to work and business as usual within the week.

Certainly, the loss of family members and friends hurt deeply back then, just as it does now. But in those days death struck so often and so early that people just accepted it as part of their lives.

Then medicine began to advance. Diseases that claimed the lives of so many began to be treatable and curable. Death didn't occur as often, and people began to live longer. People weren't confronted by grief quite so often, and death receded into the background of the collective unconscious. Folks started trying to forget the inevitability of death.

A second reason why we avoid any confrontation with death and grief is that, put simply, death is scary and grief is painful. There is so much about the process of dying that we don't understand. The fear of the unknown, and our ignorance of what happens on the other side, are major factors in shaping our attitudes about death.

Also, we are a pleasure-oriented society. We glorify the beautiful, the young, the healthy, the happy. And we frantically pursue "the good life." Such bleak subjects as death and grief are to be avoided.

But death and grief remain realities with which we must reckon. Unless we live in a sterile atmosphere free of relationships, every one of us must eventually confront grief.

Fortunately, we have shifted from a kind of John Wayne stoicism to an attitude of openness about our feelings. We encourage each other to share burdens and to verbalize the feelings of guilt, anger, loneliness, and other by-products of grief. We recognize that this is the best way to deal honestly with grief and to move quickly into the business of getting on with living.

Our problem becomes: How do we do this after having suppressed such feelings as long as we have? How do we talk with people in grief without saying something "wrong"? How can we go to those about whom we care and really help them through their darkest times? How do we put the word "dead" back into the lexicon of life?

As you will see in this book, anyone can speak effectively to a friend in grief. The basic rules are simple, and in most cases effective grief work may be done with the help of friends and neighbors. The operative word is "caring." Unless you say something drastically wrong (discussed in chapter 3), the gift of your presence can do more to ease the hurting than anything else you have to offer. The biggest obstacle we must overcome in doing good grief work is our initial reluctance. Once we jump in and show our willingness to sit with our grieving friends through their spirits' coldest winters, the rest is relatively easy.

Be warned at this point that this is not a book of formula sayings for every imagined grief situation. *What Can I Say* simply outlines some of the basic principles necessary to place us in the circle of someone else's grief when we are needed there.

Much of the material in this book is drawn from my own experience as a grieving person. It is written out of my own pain and the learnings I received from that pain. I believe it is an honest book. After my own grief journeys, I became much more sensitive to other care-needers as I sought to fulfill the role of care-giver. Now I know how grief-anger feels as well as the seemingly overwhelming feeling of grief-panic. I know that, in the case of terminal illness, the grief starts long before the patient ever dies. Now I know how sensitive bereaved people can be and how easily they differentiate honest caring from the polite emptiness of insincerity. I know that much of grief's pain goes away with time. I know what experiences were most helpful to me in my own bereavement. I believe they will help others.

Based on the information gleaned from my own experience as a grieving person, I know what works for *most* people in *most* situations. I have seen this work time and again as I have worked with others in grief.

I could not have written this book without a firsthand knowledge of how grief feels. I believe that one can be helpful and effective in helping the grieving without having gone through a bereavement of one's own (although, in fact, there are very few such inexperienced people).

It is my hope that after reading this book, you can and will try gamely to talk about death and grief honestly. I hope that "death" will cease to be a four-letter word for you. Of course, there's no point in dwelling on the subject at every conversational opportunity; that's not normal, either. But one of the most difficult feelings experienced by the bereaved is the sense of being abandoned at the time they most need the strength and support of the people around them. With the ideas contained in this book, you should never again have to choose between presence and abandonment when a friend calls for help.

I hope you enjoy this book and get some effective use from it. We are all in this together, and if we can help each other when the need arises, we will all be happier, stronger, and spiritually healthier.

Live well!

1

We All Grieve, and That's Okay— Isn't It?

A definite nip of fall was in the air. The wind rustled the leaves in the trees and some, whose time had come, floated to the ground and swept up the street. Darkness came perceptibly earlier than it had the preceding week, and there was no denying the fact that come Saturday, people in the neighborhood would begin buttoning down their homes and gardens against the approach of winter. But for now, it was a pleasant fall night.

In the middle of the block, one house was brightly lit. Cars parked along the street pointed toward the house and on any other evening, one might have surmised that a dinner party or a welcome home celebration was in progress.

17

Not this night. The lack of conversation among persons entering the house, along with the stiff and uncomfortable way they made their way to the front door hinted at something ominous.

Inside the house a woman sat on the davenport; numb, wordless, in shock. Her youngest daughter was crying in the bedroom, emerging only to answer the summons of the doorbell.

The husband and father of the house had just died. Wife and daughter had just returned from the hospital where a grim doctor had assured them that everything possible was done to save the man's life. Despite that, the damage to the backside of the heart was so extensive that no machine or bank of skill could reverse the devastation of the heart attack.

Amidst her shock, the new widow somehow made phone calls—to her pastor, to her closest neighborhood friend and to the son and daughter who lived with their own families in adjoining states. They, in turn, called others so that slowly the message spread that a father/golf partner/business associate/neighbor/friend was dead. Suddenly. Grotesquely. No riding off into the sunset. For him, it was coming home and sitting in the easy chair, complaining of indigestion. Then the searing pain, the fire that started in his chest and boiled up to race down his left arm. The feeling of slow suffocation, gasping, eyes opened wide as if somehow they could take in more air. Face turning purple and finally pitching out of the chair onto the floor. And she saw it all.

Fumbling at the telephone, dialing 911. Lights and sirens, flashes of orange on the jackets of the paramedics. Following the ambulance with a terrified daughter in the family Ford. A lifetime of waiting compressed into forty minutes and finally the grim-faced doctor walking out to the wife and daughter, the sag of his shoulders more eloquent than any words he could say.

And now, back home, friends begin to come in and surround the new widow with their presence. Some bring food. One becomes the self-appointed phone-sitter; another answers the door. Neighbors who saw the ambulance earlier now see the cars and they begin to head toward the brightly lit house in the middle of the block.

In the house, the conversation is muted. People stand in clumps around the living room and the dining room, at a loss for something to say. Occasionally, one or another of the visitors drifts self-consciously toward the widow, but then veers off before reaching her, leaving her to sit all alone in her shock and her grief. In months to come, long after the funeral is over and her husband has been buried, she will remember this night and it will occur to her that there were two or three friends who may have been a comfort to her, but who didn't come.

She wants to talk about what happened, but someone shushes her, pats her on the arm and says, "Don't talk about it now." A neighbor who recently moved into the neighborhood, and who is not very close to the family, assures the widow that it was God's will that her husband died; that his time had come to "be with Jesus." At this, she is filled with a rage that nearly eclipses the numbness inside her. Yet another tries that philosophical approach: "Well, you wouldn't want him back like he was, would you?" Inside, the widow feels guilty because she knows that she would gladly take him back on any terms. In the end, all of those who try to comfort her sidle away, knowing that though their intentions were basically good, their words were badly chosen.

* * * * *

By the time we become adults, nearly all of us find ourselves in a situation similar to the one just described. Unless we live like hermits, we encounter those who are

19

stricken with grief and we are cast, or we cast ourselves, in the role of the comforter, the care-giver, the emotional supporter. It is a role that most of us would gratefully avoid if we could; we're so afraid of making mistakes, of bungling the task. We genuinely fear being a hindrance rather than a help.

When I was in seminary, one of my professors, and a good friend of mine besides, had a heart attack. Fortunately, it was a mild one and not fatal, but my friend Loren spent many, many days in the hospital and recuperating at home. I never went to see him. I rationalized my avoidance by saying that he needed his rest more than he needed to see me; that he would have so much other company (he was a very popular professor, both with the students and with the rest of the faculty) that I would not be missed. Truthfully, I did not go because I was scared that I would find myself unable to say anything helpful to Loren.

My feeling was not unique. People from all walks of life report a feeling of real reluctance, if not outright fear, when confronting grief head-on. That fear is certainly grounded in reality! Hear the voice of grief:

> "You talk about grieving, boy, I tell you, there were days when I couldn't stand it, because I didn't know how to express myself. There was nobody to share that with. Loneliness—sudden loneliness—is a terrible thing. It took me a year to get through the crying and stuff that normally accompanies this. I didn't have anybody I could cry with; I didn't have anybody's chest to pound on, so to speak, and get rid of that stuff. I was alone and I think a lot of grieving is done that way."

The man who spoke those words was a young minister who, a few years earlier, went through a very sudden and painful divorce.

20

To one extent or another, we all know how grief feels. Granger Westberg, in his classic book entitled *Good Grief*, points out that grief feelings occur every time something of ours is perceived as lost. Certainly there is grief at the death of a spouse, close friend or relative. We recognize that and take it for granted. But there are many other circumstances in life that cause us to go through the same process. We are laid off from our jobs and we perceive the loss of income and a livelihood—and we feel grief. We must leave, for one reason or another, the church in which we were christened, reared and baptized. We perceive the loss of a very important family relationship—and we feel grief. Creditors foreclose on the farm that has been in the family for three generations; we perceive the loss of a way of life and a part of our heritage—and we feel grief. We graduate from high school or college and we perceive the loss of friends or good times—and we feel grief. Through accident or illness we are forced to undergo the amputation of an arm, a leg or a breast or we experience a physical disfigurement and we perceive the loss of mobility and all the benefits that our society bestows upon "the beautiful people"—and we feel grief. We discover that the partners with whom we have invested time, money and emotional energy to start a new business have conspired to cheat us out of our rightful portion of that business and we perceive the loss of trust, friendship and camaraderie—and we feel grief. We end a relationship with someone special and we perceive the loss of what is most important to us—and we feel grief. A pet runs away or is killed—and we feel grief.

As Westberg says, "We face minor grief almost daily in some situation or another,"[1] so we know how it feels. We know that, under normal conditions, the death of a spouse, parent or close friend elicits more grief than the loss of a job or graduation from high school. Therefore, when we encounter a situation in which someone we know is grieving,

21

we tend to shy away from that person almost instinctively. We do this because we would rather not open ourselves up to sharing the pain and because we feel incompetent and woefully inadequate in response to their grief.

Let me relate how all this crystallized in my mind. I am an ordained minister in the Christian Church (Disciples of Christ). I have been engaged in full-time pastoral ministry for almost a decade and in that short time I have already worked with dozens of families as they experienced grief. I read books on the dynamics of grief, I saw films, I role-played in pastoral care classes and I served as a student chaplain at the University of Kentucky Medical Center, among other things. With that training, I was able to emerge a fairly competent "technician"; that is, I knew the kinds of things that should and shouldn't be said, the protocol for handling death situations, where to look for funeral resources and the process of active listening during pastoral counseling. But even then, I really didn't *feel* much depth in my work when I was called upon to work with a family (the phrase "work with" is deliberately chosen, for at that point it wasn't much more than doing a job). It isn't that I am unfeeling or insensitive, just that I had experienced no first-hand grief of my own and was therefore unable to relate to people who were hurting.

To be sure, there were individual instances where I felt a strong emotional attachment to the people who died. In the course of a long illness, we would have become friends. The first funeral at which I officiated was that of a young girl from our congregation who was killed in a car wreck. Just two weeks before, her church family and I had celebrated her graduation from high school. That was a tough funeral, but I remember my emotional reactions being eclipsed by my concern for doing "the right thing" in all the circumstances of that situation.

For the most part, I was insulated from my own grief by the rationalization that, after all, the deceased person was

22

not a member of my family and therefore I was not compelled to feel too badly when an acquaintance died. I had not experienced a death in my own family circle. Then, on a Friday in September 1980, my mother called us in Nebraska to tell me that X-rays and other tests had revealed a sizeable mass in my father's right lung. "It could be anything," Mom said, "probably an infected lymph node." We both knew that while it *could* be an infected lymph node, it most likely was lung cancer.

A week passed and Mom called again. Dad had seen the doctors at University Hospitals in Iowa City, Iowa and they confirmed that there was, indeed, a cancer present in Dad's body. Furthermore, they found that the cancer had advanced so far that surgery was ruled out. As one doctor rather glibly told him, "If we were to remove it surgically, we'd have to take off the whole top of your body." They did assure him, however, that with chemotherapy and radiation treatments, the chances of a five-year survival were very good. The doctors suggested that Dad was a good candidate for experimental new treatment program having to do with nutrition and something else.

I have not yet seen the book which contains an adequate description of the feelings that accompany news like that—a description accurate enough to be meaningful to the reader. I have read things like, "We were shocked . . . we were stunned . . . we were numb," but those statements are not nearly descriptive enough.

When you receive the news of terminal illness in the family, your body physically reacts. The mind temporarily blows its circuits and shuts off, sometimes for a few moments; sometimes for days or weeks. The heart seems to expand rapidly, almost as though there is an explosion within it, and then it settles down to a steady thudding, seemingly on "auto-pilot," rather than its normal pumping actions. There is a sinking feeling in all the organs located underneath the diaphragm and there is a sensation something like having ice cold water run through your intestines. All this happens in about three seconds.

After that, thoughts remain muddled and a dreamlike aura pervades every waking moment. You go through the days disoriented and yet at the same time you become acutely conscious of everything that everyone else says about the illness. I guess it's that way because, either consciously or subconsciously, you're desperately eager to hear words that will reverse the process and make the illness go away so that everything will be okay again as it was before. All else becomes irrelevant and unimportant to you. You appear to others to be distracted and disinterested unless the conversation centers on the illness, at which time you become manic as you talk about your loved one's condition and what you know about how the disease generally progresses. And then the shock wears off, and then, O God, then comes the pain.

As the initial shock of the news wore off, the realities and the prognosis of the situation began to sink in with the subtlety of a brutal meeting in a back alley. At first, the doctors made very optimistic sounds. Chemotherapy showed good results in cases like Dad's, and radiation treatments were highly effective with the type of cancer he had, oat-cell carcinoma of the lung. Dad made plans to have the next Miller family reunion in the town in which they had lived for just six months before all this happened. He made plans to continue his ministry on a part-time basis until the cancer was treated and consigned to a state of remission.

But then the doors began to close. Dad didn't meet the qualifications for the experimental program after all. The one chemotherapy treatment he had made him profoundly ill, and while he lost all his hair, the tumor ran on unchecked. His blood count was lowered by that one treatment so that no further treatments were possible. The radiation program, ten treatments in ten days, seemed to retard the growth of the tumor somewhat, but it also caused third degree burns on the inside of Dad's throat so that he couldn't swallow food. When the doctors saw that nothing seemed to be helping, they politely but definitely conveyed the message that there was nothing more they could do for him; he was referred to a private physician in Iowa City.

For six months, we watched Dad gradually deteriorate until he died on a Sunday morning in March 1981. For all the months preceding Dad's death and for a couple of years afterward, we lived with a pain that had no remedy. At times, it was nearly unbearable and I still feel really badly when I think about the nights that Dad must have sat in his reclining chair in the living room, alone with his thoughts in the wee hours of the morning. Before the final stage of the cancer, he was a night person, often staying up to watch television or read. After the cancer was discovered and the treatments failed, I wonder what Dad thought about and how he felt during those lonely nights when he would sit up alone. I imagined how I would feel if I were in his position and my pain for Dad was very great. Later on, we found out that he used those times to record messages to all of us: Mom, my sister Karla, my wife Evie, our kids Sarah and Seth and me. He would also write letters to us and spend much time reading his Bible and praying. I believe that it wasn't so much prayer borne of desperation or an attempt to bargain with God as it was a form of meditative preparation.

At any rate, our grief process was in full-swing during that time. I lost interest in virtually everything else. This was complicated by a move we made from Nebraska to Iowa, partly to be closer to my folks. Everything we did, said, thought about and lived was colored by Dad's cancer and the dynamics of grief we felt.

From the time Dad died, our healing process started. Now, years later, it still continues. Some months after Dad's death, I was thinking about the people who were helpful to me in my grief and about those who should have been helpful but, for one reason or other, were not. My brother-in-law and I were talking about grief and working with bereaved people. In the course of the conversation, he pointed out that so many of us feel helpless when it comes to dealing with grief. "I wouldn't know what to say," is the way he put it and as he said that, I remembered all the people I've encountered in the course of my work who said exactly the same thing. Before Dad died, I never knew how to respond to those people's dilemma; common sense told me that simple platitudes would be of little comfort.

But after dealing with my father's death, I can offer some practical ideas for those who find themselves in the role of care-giver to a relative, friend or acquaintance.

When people close to us are grieving, they often turn to us for emotional support whether we want them to or not. Certainly they must bear the brunt of their grief alone and handle much of their inner healing themselves; however, we can and should be there for them, which will lessen the burden considerably.

Of course we feel uncomfortable because we don't know what to say to make the other person feel better and we're even more afraid we'll blurt out something insensitive. But it is possible to be a sincere comfort to people in grief and to help them grow through that grief.

With that goal in mind, what you will *not* find in this book is a list of snappy sayings and formulae to be toted out when the situation requires them ("Case #24: When One Has Died of a Heart Attack—Say These Things . . ."). To write a book like that would be insensitive and presumptuous; it would be like putting little Band-aids on gaping spiritual wounds.

Another thing to keep in mind when reading this book is that it will not turn you into Super-Pastor, Super-Counselor or Super-Anything-Else.

The purpose of this book is to help you overcome, to some small degree, your reluctance to confront grief situations, and to say that there are certain principles or guidelines that you can follow in order to be truly helpful in almost all circumstances where grief is present.

No matter what the cause of grief may be, the stages of grief are essentially the same. However, we'll confine our discussion here to the circumstances surrounding death, since this situation produces the most stress and profound grief in its survivors.

In order to deal with grief in a meaningful and effective way, we must keep several assumptions in mind. Remember that grief is a God-given emotion. It is as normal and natural as joy, happiness, anger and love. To encounter someone in grief is to experience someone going up and down the full range of the emotional repertoire. Not to grieve, or the inability to grieve, is a sign of emotional incompleteness. Although never pleasant, grief is a part of the human condition. That's the first assumption.

The second assumption is that it is okay to grieve. Too often, we censor our feelings and repress our emotions because whatever we're feeling just doesn't seem proper or convenient. We need to remember that unexpressed grief will surface later in insidious and debilitative ways. It's okay to answer the question, "How are you today?" with an emphatic "Lousy!" When we're with someone in grief, we need to be more accepting and less uncomfortable. The expression of grief is a very therapeutic physiologic function; bottling up grief can damage us physically as well as emotionally.

The third assumption is that human beings are social creatures. We are made for relationships and community, and it is natural to want emotional support when we are in grief. There is nothing weak about reaching out to others for emotional and spiritual support or accepting that support when it is offered. Nor is it an invasion of privacy or any kind of imposition to offer emotional and spiritual support to someone who is grieving.

The fourth assumption is an especially important one: in giving support to one who is in grief, the intention is not to make everything all better or to erase the sadness being expressed. Nothing will ever make things exactly as they were before; as much as we'd like it to be so, there are not magic words to take the pain completely away.

Keeping these assumptions in mind will enable us to give support in grief situations with confidence and effectiveness. Although grief is difficult, the guidelines presented in the rest of this book should enable you to answer for yourself the question, "What Can I Say?"

Notes

1. Granger Westberg, *Good Grief.* Fortress Press, 1971, p. 16.

2

The Gift of Presence

During the relatively short time I have been a minister, I've seen the face of grief many times: on the family members of the girl killed in the Kentucky car wreck; and at Eppley Airfield in Omaha as a brother and sister broke the news to their mother that their father had died in his sleep the night before. She had just returned from a visit to her parents. I'll never forget the way her expression changed from one of welcome greeting to shock and horror as they let her know that she was now a widow.

I saw the face of grief on the family of a man who had gone out hunting one afternoon. He'd been depressed and was on tranquilizers. His brother drove out to the deer stand to pick him up for supper as the sun's last rays hit the countryside. As the brother got out of the car, he heard a gunshot and shortly thereafter, he found his brother's body leaning against the tree. Some theorized that as the young man got down out of the tree, his rifle slipped from his arm, discharging and killing him instantly; others said it was obviously suicide. It didn't really matter either way; he was dead.

Many times I grieved with families gathered around hospital beds as the chest of a loved one rose and fell for the last time, concluding courageous battles with cancer or heart disease.

Whenever I was in a situation playing the role of the pastor, the care-giver, the source of emotional and spiritual support, I was very conscious of that role and because I really cared about the people, I tried my best to do and say things that might be genuinely helpful to them in their time of grief. I tried to do and say things that would give both comfort and support and provide a basis for spiritual growth in the future. I used words and silences that were carefully chosen. I consciously avoided clichés and platitudes because I knew that if the words sounded empty to me, they would surely sound empty and insincere to those I was trying to help. Sometimes there seemed to be nothing helpful that could be said in that situation, nothing meaningful to say, so I would just sit with the family, maybe just holding a hand, feeling helpless and inadequate in the silence.

Whenever possible, I would make the funeral services personal, but there were times, of course, when this was impossible, such as the time when I had the graveside service of a man who had died in Ohio and was returned to Nebraska for the interment. I remember in the case of a man who had died of abdominal cancer, we used his favorite 8-track tape recording as prelude music for the service. It so happened that the music was played by Hawaiian steel guitars—a little unorthodox, I admit, but very meaningful to the family. I would always use carefully chosen scripture readings that in some way pertained to the life of the one who had died.

Remember that at this point in my ministry, I had had no personal experience with grief. I was working on the basis of what I had been told was the proper way to give pastoral care in death situations, along with what I thought might be helpful. It seemed to work. After the funerals were over, the families would tell me that I had been a real help to them. They seemed sincere and I was flattered.

Then Dad got lung cancer and I found myself on the other side of grief. I was no longer the care-giver, the source of strength, the miracle worker or the pastoral superman that I had envisioned myself to be. I became a little kid again; scared, confused, ineffective and desperately reaching out for help from someone—anyone—because my Daddy was dying and I didn't know how to stop it. I was the one needing ministry rather than the one giving it.

At first, I tried to minister to myself. I tried to tell myself the same kinds of things I had been saying to others, but it definitely was *not* working for me. Everything I had ever said about God's love and presence in such situations seemed hollow. The words of hope did no good and I remained essentially in a state of hopelessness. My prayers were grounded in fear and confusion rather than strength and confidence.

The fact that I apparently failed to minister to myself caused a self-confidence crisis that almost made me give up the ministry. How, I reasoned, could I minister to others if I couldn't even help myself? For about a month, I had no desire to preach, counsel, make hospital calls or home-bound visitations or do any of the other things contained within my pastoral job description. I realized for the first time in my life what the psalmist was talking about when he wrote of living in the "Pit" (Psalm 103:4). But then an interesting thing began to happen.

31

We were blessed with several friends who did not hesitate to come around and offer their services as "ministers." Most of them were not professional ministers, although a few were. They were all, however, sensitive and caring, loving and concerned. They seemed to know just what to do for my wife Evie and me at the time. They were present and visible. They made sure to include us in their social activities even when we didn't feel like socializing. They were patient with me when, in the midst of a casual time together, I would steer the conversation—almost against my will— around to the subjects of cancer and Dad's illness. They stayed around when I became really obnoxious and acted in such a way that even I didn't want to be around myself. They reassured us of their love for us and God's love for us; when they offered their words of comfort, those words worked. To have Alan and Freeda and Tom and Beth and Gary and Larry tell me of God's presence was to experience that presence in a tangible way.

I'm convinced that the effectiveness of comforting words lies not in the words themselves but in who offers them and in what way. I realized that in my pastoral work before Dad's illness, I really had been helpful to those families in grief, primarily because I had been present during their hurting times.

The gift of presence is perhaps the most important element in helping people in grief. To be willing to venture out of safe territory onto the dangerous emotional turf of another's bereavement demonstrates a very speical kind of caring. That caring is a strengthening influence in and of itself. To go to someone who is hurting and feeling totally without inner resources is to say nonverbally to that person, "I am willing to give you myself—my feelings, my patience, my strength and anything else I have so that together we can work through this time. I am willing to share your pain; to walk this hard road with you and face whatever peril your problems present to me." An eloquent statement like that is made without words, just by a person's showing up.

A friend of mine who is involved in Alcoholics Anonymous reminds me of a saying that members of that group live by: "We can handle what I can't." That is the essence of the gift of presence! The first principle in helping those you love through their grieving times to be physically present with them if at all possible. Next door, across town, in the next county—those distances are no problem. But what about the friend who lives in the next state or across the country? The efficacy of your being physically present with them becomes dependent upon a lot of things, not the least of which is the strength of the bond(s) you have with the grieving person(s). I have friends in Oklahoma with whom I would be with immediately if they needed me. Then again, there are people who live not nearly so far away who would probably be just as comfortable with a note or a phone call. The gift of presence is where healing begins in the grief process.

Shortly after we had moved from Falls City, Nebraska, to Jefferson, Iowa, my wife and I were attending an annual regional meeting for ministers. Although I had been away from the region for a few years, I still knew most of the ministers in one way or another. Over the course of the three-day meeting, several of these ministers came to me to ask about my dad. I was grateful for this, because I needed to talk about what was happening. I thought that this was an especially skilled and empathetic group of concerned listeners who could help me sort things out.

"How's your dad getting along?" they would typically ask. "Oh, so-so," I would answer. "He hadn't been able to take more than one chemotherapy treatment because of the changes in his blood chemistry; he tried radiation around Christmas time, but that burnt his throat shut. Right now,

33

he's pretty much holding his own, doesn't have too much pain most of the time. He's at home in North Liberty [Iowa], staying at his apartment while he can; he really doesn't want to go back to the hospital."

My wife Evie noticed long before I did that right after I said, "Oh, so-so," the ministers' eyes would glaze over and they would begin shifting from foot to foot until a graceful exit could be made. After this happened several times, it finally dawned on me that while these ministers made inquiries about Dad, it was more to be polite than to render much emotional support to me. Dad's cancer was nothing more than a conversation-starter, something to talk about to fill up the silences. The realization that these colleagues did not want to share their gift of presence with me was a very hard thing to handle. Now, years after Dad's passing, I still feel some resentment toward those who extended their gifts of presence by asking about Dad but who then snatched them away.

I asked myself why they would do such a thing. Perhaps they were made painfully aware of their own mortality by the knowledge of such misfortune so close to home. Or maybe in their eagerness to escape their congregations, relax and loosen up a bit, they didn't really want to hear any more bad news or deal with any more grief.

I must emphasize that not all the ministers at that meeting were reluctant to give me their gift of presence. There were a few who had known Dad for years and who were most helpful, genuine and sincere in their inquiries about Dad. These people know who they are and they should know that they have my continuing gratitude.

For the others, I can at least say this: Their actions taught me a very important lesson. When we offer our gift of presence to one in grief, the offer must be sincere. We must be willing to follow through with the emotional investment if we are the ones to make the initial offer. Otherwise it's better to talk about the weather or anything else, rather than to give the bereaved person the false hope of emotional support.

Shortly after Dad's cancer was discovered, my parents had to move from their parsonage to an apartment about a hundred miles away, closer to the hospital. Even after they moved, many people from their congregation extended the gift of presence to my folks. One day, however, Mom got a call from a woman in the congregation. After talking about other things, the woman said, "By the way, I won't be coming up to see you. I can't bear to see Bob the way he is; I want to remember him as he was." What my parents inferred from this message was, "I am so concerned about my own feelings that I don't want to see Bob, all bald and bloated and dying." Not only did this person decline to give my folks the gift of her presence, but she also hurt them by virtually abandoning them when they needed their friends the most.

Elisabeth Kübler-Ross found through her studies of terminally ill people that many reported a feeling of isolation and abandonment during the times their diseases progressed. This was one of the most unpleasant aspects of the dying process. In part, that feeling of isolation is due to attitudes like those held by the woman who called my mother. If you don't want to see someone, yet you still want to express your concern for her or him, it's quite all right to lend your support through a card, a note or a thoughtful telephone call.

When we know of someone who is grieving, and we decide to give that person emotional support, we must, to the best of our ability, make ourselves physically and emotionally available. We have to become vulnerable to the same kinds of pain and hurt that the person in grief is experiencing. We need to realize that more important than our words is our presence, and unless what we say is totally tasteless, the help we give lies not so much in what we say, but in the fact that we are there.

In the Old Testament book of Job, we read of a man who had it all; wealth, influence, a good family and health. He possessed all of the things that made life complete and good.

Then he lost it. First went the crops and cattle, then Job's children and finally his health. No one in this or any other time had any more valid cause for grief than did Job. He donned sackcloth and ashes, the traditional garb of mourning and sat in the gutter pondering his fate. Three of Job's friends came to be with him then:

> Now when Job's three friends heard of all this evil that was upon him, they came each one from his own place, Eliphaz the Termanite, and Bildad the Shuhite and Zophar the Naamathite; for they had made an appointment together to come to condole with him and to comfort him (Job).
>
> And when they looked from afar off and saw him [disfigured] beyond recognition; they lifted up their voices and wept; and they each one tore his robe and they cast dust over their heads toward the heavens.
>
> So they sat down with [Job] on the ground seven days and seven nights, and none spoke a word to him, for they saw that his grief and pain were very great. (Job 2:11-13, Amplified Bible)

This is a very significant passage. Notice that the three friends, Eliphaz, Bildad and Zophar, "made an appointment" together to come and condole Job. Apparently, they had heard of Job's plight, communicated among themselves and recognized the importance of their gift of presence to Job at that time. It was an unselfish act; they had no ulterior motives, for they were aware that Job had lost everything. They knew that Job had reached a point where he needed physical and emotional support which could only come from friends who cared.

Notice, too, that the three friends identified with Job's grief. When they saw him, they suffered such spasms of feeling for Job that they engaged in traditional expressions of grieving; rending their clothes and throwing dust over their heads. Their genuine grief was evident as they lifted their voices and wept.

Perhaps most significant is that when the friends reached Job, they sat down with him "and none spoke a word" for seven days and seven nights, because they saw the extent of his grief. Even now, thousands of years later, this passage still stands as a near-perfect illustration of the importance of the gift of presence.

A minister friend of mine relates this experience he had while he was a student.

I was serving as a director of youth ministries for a church of about 900 members. The senior pastor was gone and a call came in that a couple in our church had a son who just committed suicide. These people, you know, the grandparent image, just super folks; very good Christians and all that, their son had just killed himself. I remember the call came in and I thought, "My God, how do I deal with this?" Here I was, a student, and I thought "What do I say to these people?" because they were "super-Christians," you know, the kind of people you'd call on if you wanted a good pastoral prayer. Boy, he could pray and you could feel it coming from the inside.

So I went to the house and the family was there and the only thing I could do was sit down and cry with them. And I walked away from that afterwards, thinking that if the senior pastor had been there, what words of wisdom would he have given? But we both went together the next day and he didn't do anything; it was just the idea of our being there. Because there isn't anything you're going to say to make it all right and that situation was unique because it was suicide and when you're dealing with suicide, you're dealing with some pretty heavy questions. There's nothing you can say to the family of a suicide; there's just nothing to be said.

More and more, people experienced in grief work recognize the importance of the gift of presence. When we recognize it and can lend it to those who are grieving, we can help them immeasurably. Even if we are not with them physically, we can send them a card or a note or we communicate with them by telephone. We can extend the gift of presence and in so doing, start those grieving on the road to recovery.

3

What Not to Say to People in Grief

In the Old Testament, we find the bittersweet story of Job. As mentioned in the chapter before, Job certainly had reason to grieve. Within a very short time, he had lost his home, his family and his health. Job was left with his life and very little more. Three of Job's friends—Eliphaz, Bildad and Zophar—gathered around Job and attempted to assuage his grief. For the first seven days and nights, nobody said anything; each just lent Job the gift of his presence. So far, the friends had done well; they seemed to be a source of comfort and support for Job. Then Job started to talk, and the plot thickened.

Job bared his soul and tried to find some reason for his predicament. Through his soliloquies, he vented his feelings of desolation, pain and bewilderment. In response, the three friends answered Job. Somehow, they felt as if they must say something—anything—so they answered Job with well-constructed arguments. They answered Job with appeals to his human nature ("You think you've got problems? Everybody's got problems!"). They answered Job with platitudes and cliches ("Since God rewards the righteous and punishes the wicked, you must have done something to make him mad!"). In the end, Job said, in effect, "I've heard all this before and it doesn't help." Finally, he dismissed Eliphaz, Bildad and Zophar with the words, "The comfort you give is only torment" (Job 16:2).

Without a doubt, the three friends were well-intentioned. The fact that they made an appointment to come and be with Job speaks well of their desire to help him through his calamitous times. In sitting with Job in silence, they lent him their gift of presence and yet, in trying to comfort Job, they said precisely the wrong things.

Perhaps we in our time are not so different! How many times have we fallen prey to the "Open-Mouth-Insert-Foot" syndrome, in which we say something that comes out sounding exactly the opposite of what we meant to say? And how many times have we avoided contact with people in grief because we were afraid that whatever we might say would be inappropriate? A counselor friend tells me that often people run away from the very ones who can help them. Perhaps it is also true that we avoid those to whom we can give the most help.

It doesn't have to be that way! In addition to our gift of presence, the most important thing we can bring to a friend or relative in grief is a rudimentary sensitivity to their plight and their feelings. This sensitivity, at its very least, should cause us to question carefully all that we say *before* we offer it in the name of comfort. Too often, we find ourselves parroting back something to bereaved persons simply because those are the things we have heard before. Seldom do we really think about the things we say and yet we find that some of the ritualistic patter we lay on grieving people is not only unhelpful, but it also may be counterproductive.

While this is not a book of things to say, I am taking the liberty of including some things *not* to say. For instance:

"That's okay, he/she led a long, full life." My grandfather died. After an extended period of declining health, he suffered a massive stroke which left him in a coma for a week before he succumbed. He was 81.

Some of my earliest memories involve Granddad. I spent the first three years of my life living in his house while my own father was at sea with the Navy. He always made me feel important. He was my first hero. He literally taught me how to walk and to this day, I carry my left shoulder higher than my right because that's the way Granddad walked after years of shoveling coal on railroad engines.

So, anyway, he died. Many people expressed their condolences to me and my family and while all of these people were genuinely concerned, there were some who said something like, "Oh well, then, he had a long full life, didn't he?" That was a fact, yes, but the message made us feel as though because of the fact that he lived 81 years, we should not feel badly; to grieve for him now would somehow be unfair to those who had lost younger loved ones.

"He had a long full life." We hear it so often and I'm sure that I've said it a time or two myself. But if we really stop to think about what is implied in that statement, it seems to be contrary to all that we have been taught about living as people of God and followers of Jesus Christ. Many times in the gospel, Jesus made reference to the worth and value of all persons no matter what their age, station in life or physical condition. He said things like, ". . . if God so clothes the grass of the field which today is alive and tomorrow is thrown into the oven, will he not much more clothe you, O you of little faith" (Matthew 6:30). Time and again,

Jesus demonstrated in his encounters with people that they were indeed important. If we live with and love someone for many years, it seems natural that their value to us would increase rather than decrease as time goes by. When someone we love is gone, how callous it is for us to dismiss them from our memories with the rationalization that since they have lived for many years, they don't really deserve as much grief when they die; that since their "time is up," we don't have to hurt—indeed, we shouldn't hurt when they go away.

Perhaps it has something to do with our desire to escape the pain that accompanies grief. We may be seeking to fool ourselves by saying: If I rationalize away the importance of this loved one's death to me life—if I make his/her passing less important to me—then maybe it won't hurt as much.

It didn't work like that for me. I found that the expression, "Well, he had a long full life," may have been true, but it wasn't particularly helpful to hear. In fact, I resented those well-meant attempts to make me feel better through the minimization of Granddad's importance.

Now, some might say, "Well, at least the passing of an older person is not as tragic as that of a younger person." Interestingly, as the same time Granddad died, so did the husband of my wife's best friend. A victim of Hodgkin's disease, he died at the age of 31. I had the opportunity to compare the two death experiences and I found that both hurt terribly. There was an element of tragedy in the death of the younger man that was not present in Granddad's death, but both experiences created grief. Comparing deaths on the basis of the victim's age is like comparing apples and oranges. While there are a few similarities, each circumstance has its own particular source of pain—its own particular dynamics. Each person's death is unique.

The same thing can be said for situations other than death. We tend to try to minimize difficult situations by reasoning, "It could be worse." This attitude does not console people in grief! To the person who is bereaved—for whatever reason—the cause of that bereavement is all that matters. To say, "It could be worse," is to elicit the unspoken response, "That's what you think! How could you know?"

If we love someone, age has nothing to do with the way we feel when he dies. There is a woman in my church whom I love like my own grandmother. She is somewhere in her eighties and she lives each day to its fullest. She is the kind of Christian who has realized death's eventuality and has talked with me about her funeral plans. She greets the prospect of death as the door that will lead her from this life to a greater everlasting life and when the time comes for her to die, she will face it fearlessly and joyously. She is pushing ninety years of age and though I've known her only five, when she dies I will grieve for her the same as I would for a member of my own family. To say, "That's all right, she had a good long life," is to minimize her worth at a time when she will be sorely missed.

"*It was God's will.*" Read this passage from the Gospel of John:

As [Jesus] passed by, he saw a man blind from his birth. And his disciples asked him, "Rabbi, who sinned, this man or his parents that he was born blind?" Jesus answered, "It was not that this man sinned, or his parents, but that the works of God might be made manifest in him. We must work the works of him who sent me, while it is day; night comes when no one can work. As long as I am in the world, I am the light of the world" (John 9:1-5).

Jesus' disciples asked a question which reflects the popular theology of the time. It was the general consensus among religious persons that God rewarded those who were godly by granting them prosperity, and God punished those who were not. Centuries later, that philosophy persists despite what both Job and Jesus taught. No matter what some believe, we can *not* easily discern the will of God. From the study of scripture, we might easily conclude that God intends for us to live long, healthy, abundant lives here on earth. We might point to the passage in the book of Lamentations which says, "For the Lord will not cast off forever. But though he causes [allows] grief, he does not willingly grieve nor afflict the sons of men" (Lamentations 3:33).

People often say, "It was God's will," with the intention of consoling the bereaved. The net result, however, is to cause anger at God for taking away the loved one. To be sure, anger is a normal part of the grieving process, but the blame—the target of the anger—is misdirected.

I have heard this said at a child's funeral. I became so angry I had to leave the room before I spoke intemperately myself. God does *not* will children to die capriciously. He does not have a huge cruise liner for which he must make up a passenger list for people of all ages. God takes no delight in tragic practical jokes. Usually, when this sentiment is expressed, it goes something like, "God just needed some beautiful flowers for his garden, so he plucked little Johnny for his bouquet." Grief is a time when people need all the support they can get from friends, family and God himself. To assert that "It was God's will" that someone died is to cut off the possibility of divine support during the most crucial period of bereavement.

Like the disciples in the Gospel of John, we make the assertion, "It was God's will" with the understanding that we are suffering because of some sin we have committed and this is God's revenge. Scripture tells us that this is not how God works. I am the parent of two children and I love them more than my own life. A thought that terrifies me is that something might happen to them. If something does, I

44

can't—and won't—believe that the God I love and serve is the cause of their misfortune and mine. To be sure, God would be a part of the situation, but not as the cause of the grief. To say, "It was God's will," to the parents of a dead child is not only in bad taste, but blasphemous!

Leslie Weatherhead has written a book entitled *The Will of God* in which he posits the thesis that there are three natures to God's will: the intentional will, the circumstantial will and ultimate will. Weatherhead says that it is God's intentional will that everyone live long and healthy in the land in which God has placed them. However, sometimes the circumstances of life force a decision to continue or end a life. An example of circumstantial will would be a brain injury from a car accident or a cancer that has advanced too far to be treated. God's ultimate will is exercised when the spirit survives the death of the body and moves into the next phase of life.

Given this arrangement, it may well be possible that the death of someone at any given time is the circumstantial will of God. But to dwell on that part of God's will is to forget all about his intentional and ultimate wills. At any rate, it really does no good to emphasize the will of God when talking with someone in grief. Even when the circumstances of life seem abundantly clear to us and we seem to see God working in our lives, we must remember that, "His ways are not our ways," and there is an element of mystery that must preclude us from saying with certainty, "It was God's will."

"*Your/his/her faith wasn't strong enough.*" This insensitive and absurd statement has caused untold damage to so many grieving families. Remember the time Jesus got word about the illness of his friend Lazarus? He finished up his business and then went on to Bethany where Lazarus had, in the meantime, died. Mary said to Jesus, "If you had only been here, Lazarus wouldn't have died" (John 11:32). This kind of statement places the blame for a person's death on his survivors!

45

I believe that God heals disease or injury in one of three ways: directly, with no other intervention; indirectly, through the health care profession; and finally, through death. To insinuate that someone has died because of a lack of faith is to impose our wishes and desires on a situation which may, for all we know, be well in hand.

A former acquaintance told me during the visitation period for my dad that had Dad's faith been stronger, ". . . we all wouldn't need to be here." Having known my father as a man of deep faith—a faith which brought him through many adversities—this thoughtless comment really angered me! This sort of statement does no good and only serves to deepen any feelings of anger or guilt in the bereaved.

"Don't talk about it now." I hear this one a lot and I think it's one of the well-intentioned statements. The rationale behind this comment seems to be: If you don't talk about it, you won't think about it and if you don't think about it, you won't feel badly. This is a logical line of reasoning, but the logic is faulty. When someone has lost a loved one or a job or marriage, it takes far more than merely discussing the weather or the local high school football team to begin to wash away the grief. There are notable exceptions, but for the most part, people want and need to talk about their grief. To relate a cataclysmic event is to get it outside oneself where it can be examined more objectively by "outsiders."

One New Year's Eve as we were preparing to celebrate the stroke of midnight, my son was bitten in the face by our family dog. The bite was a bad one and it necessitated a trip to our local hospital. The surgeons there looked at it and decided that we should take Seth on to Des Moines, where a specialist could examine him more closely and repair a severed tear duct. After admitting Seth to the hospital, I drove back home in the midst of a snowstorm that had begun while we were in the Emergency Room. The sky was just turning light as I drove into the driveway. I made arrangements for someone to take charge of my worship service (New Year's Day was Sunday this year) and then turned around and drove back to the hospital in time to accompany Seth to the operating room. It was a long, sleepless night of terrible emotional and spiritual strain.

The morning seemed to drag on as we sat alone in the waiting room. The doctor's announcement that everything went well and that Seth would be fine was such a relief that we shed tears of gratitude and exhaustion.

Afterward, I had an almost compulsive need to recount the details of the whole night to anyone who expressed the least bit of interest. I can't remember the number of times I told the story, but I do remember the time I was given the opportunity to tell it once again and I felt that doing so would be such a chore. I felt that a great weight had been lifted from my shoulders because I no longer had the need to talk about that bad experience. This was the beginning of the resurrection process from my grief.

This same dynamic is present when someone loses a loved one. Thinking back on my own experience, I realize that my need to give a complete health report on my dad to the ministers who politely asked about him was this need to verbalize my grief. It seems as if nature's emotional release valve is often our mouths. Reliving an experience through words is the means by which we can anchor ourselves emotionally and spiritually to one spot in time and from that spot move forward to a process of eventual resurrection and recovery. Many times I've sat in the living rooms of church members and listened to bereaved people tell the same story in the same words over and over again.

When people say, "Don't talk about it now," they may delay the process of emotional and spiritual healing. It is much better for us to listen actively and empathetically as they tell their personal stories. Unexpressed grief eventually expresses itself in unhealthy ways, so while the process may be painful, it is always best to verbalize feelings as soon as possible. Let the grieving process begin!

"You wouldn't want him/her back as he/she was, would you?" Surprisingly enough, the answer to that question is an emphatic, "Yes!" While it is true that death often ends a painful life, it is also true that death negates a physical presence as well. People are glad when their loved ones stop hurting, but that glimmer of gratitude is powerfully overshadowed by the pain of a loss. Ultimately, no amount of reasoning, rationalizing or theologizing can take the place of the touch of a husband's hand, the sound of a mother's voice, the distinctive flavor of a father's sense of humor or the attention and devotion that only a child can bestow upon its parents. When we do not hurt inside, we are naturally concerned about others. But when we are grieving, the only suffering we can feel is our own. To say, "You wouldn't want her back as she was, would you?" causes the bereaved person to realize, yes, I would, which only adds to the burden of guilt that is a normal part of the grieving process.

The last time I saw my dad alive was on the evening before he died. His last two weeks had been particularly difficult for him and the lung cancer had spread completely throughout his body. He was in great pain. On his doctor's advice, Mom and my sister gave him strong pain medication as often as he requested it. His hair was gone and his upper plate lay in a denture cup because he could no longer wear it. His arms and legs were emaciated while his torso was filled with fluid. He was becoming comatose. We knew his condition was terminal and yet, right up to the time my wife called and told me he had died, I held the hope that someone somewhere would cure him. Even when we know that death is imminent, we are never completely prepared for it. The statement, "You wouldn't want him back like he is," underscores the feeling of helplessness and unpreparedness in the bereaved.

48

"It's all right. You shouldn't feel badly." I truly believe that this comment is one of those merely spoken to fill up silence. Whatever the grief-producing circumstance, why should we not feel badly? A loved one had died, we have just lost our job, the decision to move has been made, we have just ended our marriage or lost a lover—all of these things grab us where we hurt and upset our emotional equilibrium. The status of our lives has been disturbed and we must begin a reorienting process to take up the slack. Most certainly it (whatever "it" may be) is *not* all right!

God has put grief into our emotional repertoire. We do ourselves a great disservice if we deny that feeling and delude ourselves into thinking that whatever happens is "all right." We do others a great disservice, as well, if we urge the same upon them. A person's feelings are unique; how he or she feels is how each feels and it is quite presumptuous of us to tell someone how that one should feel.

Some time ago, a relative had surgery to correct a pylonida cyst, a small ingrown sore on the tailbone. A couple of days after the operation, the doctor was inspecting his work, with much poking and prodding. He evidently hit a raw nerve, for Uncle Joe winced and cried, "Ouch!" The doctor looked very insulted and huffed, "That didn't hurt!" to which the patient replied, "Not you, maybe, but it hurt me like crazy!" (edited in the interest of propriety and good taste).

We become, in a sense, as arrogant as that doctor when we tell someone he or she shouldn't feel badly when that person is in grief. The comment we offer with good intentions becomes truly counterproductive.

"You're still young." This thoughtless message is reserved for widows and widowers and implies that they are suddenly incomplete without a mate, but there's still plenty of time to catch another. Mom was just fifty when Dad died. She said that such comments only confused and angered

her. She was right in the midst of recovering from the loss of the most significant person in her life; getting married again was the furthest thought from her mind.

When my friend went through a painful divorce, he spoke of his own grieving process, by noting, "There should be a period of mourning. I had people trying to set me up with a date and I wasn't ready, but I didn't have the backbone to tell them, 'No, I don't want to!'"

Grieving people need time and space to work through their grief. In its first stages, they cannot look beyond the immediate situation to the months and years ahead, nor do they particularly want to. A well-intentioned reassurance that "You're still young" also causes the grieving person to call his or her own personal worth into question. Many bereaved people report that they experience the "fifth wheel" syndrome when socializing with friends. This bit of counsel reinforces the notion that a single person has less personal worth than one who is half of a couple. While it is true that our society is changing its attitude toward single people, we are, by and large, a couple-oriented society. To say, "You're still young," (don't worry, you'll get someone else) emphasizes not only the abrupt switch from partnership to autonomy, but also sends a message to the bereaved that his or her social acceptability has been placed on hold for the time being.

"If there's anything I can do, let me know." I used to say this all the time until I experienced the comment from the other side and thought about it. When genuinely offered from one friend to another, it is an affirmation of the highest level of trust that exists between two people. Too often, however, it's used as a cleanup phrase by people who want to escape the bereaved. Then the offer is shallow and insincere. Remember that the ears of grief are fine-tuned to insincerity and in this instance, if your offer does not come from the heart, the words are better left unsaid.

50

Such a comment can produce another problem for the bereaved. To say, in effect, "Tell me what to do," is to put the ball in the grieving person's court—right where it doesn't belong. The grieving mind doesn't function very well in the detail mode. Attempts to think of something for a care-giver to do just compounds the mental and emotional strain of the grief experience.

Then there are the people who will not ask for assistance, even when it is offered. My mother was reared to be a very independent person and since Dad's death, she has had to learn to reach out to my sister and me for support.

If we really want to help someone in grief, we should make a specific offer of assistance. It's easier to accept and harder to turn down and it relieves the bereaved of the burden of thinking of something for us to do.

In general, people are not irresponsibly insensitive. The people who were helpful to me far outnumbered those who weren't. As I said before, it was so important to me that my friends gave me the gift of their presence that what they actually said now slips my mind. Those who hesitate about what to say to a bereaved person may be evincing the very sensitivity that is required of a good care-giver. The key lies in thinking about what you say *before* you say it. You might take the permissible silent time with a grieving friend to ask yourself: Is what I'm about to say going to enable my hurting friend to express his or her feelings honestly or might it build yet another wall that he or she will have to go through on his or her road to recovery? Before extending care to someone in grief, we should reflect on the types of things that would be most helpful and least helpful to us if we were in grief. A moment's consideration should provide a good basis from which we can talk to people in grief.

4

How to Talk to People in Grief

Wouldn't it be great if all we needed to get through life were a few glib phrases, a few pat sayings? Relationships would be so comfortable. Our social anxiety level would drop to nil and life would be so easy! But as we know all too well, life isn't easy and it takes more than just a correct formula to make relationships work. There's no way we can plug Saying Number 15-A into Situation Number 15-B. When we try that, the result is invariably phony and contrived. As mentioned before, people in grief are tuned in to insincerity. They have been tremendously insulted already and their guard is up against further hurt. In many cases, grief fosters an over-sensitivity to pain and any gesture which is even remotely perceived as insincere may be a negative influence in the journey back to wholeness. We know this; we've experienced it ourselves. That's part of what intimidates us about relating to bereaved people. We think we have to do and say the things that will restore the emotional injury to perfect health—to fix it—without resorting to clichés and platitudes.

Now hear this: *Nothing* we can do or say will reverse a grief situation. There are no magic words that will make it all better. When talking to people in grief, the main objective is to try to begin a healing process very much like that of a surgical patient. Think about it: Grief and surgery have many parallels. Surgery is to the body what grief is to the mind and spirit. In the days immediately following an operation, the incision is raw and sore. The hurt is incredible! But concerned care-givers can help the patient manage the pain until healthy scar tissue forms. In time, the pain subsides and the patient returns to his normal routine. The scar remains, however, a constant reminder of the time when the body was traumatically insulted by the surgeon's scalpel.

Grief is just like that. At first, the pain is sharp and fierce. But the tender ministrations of friends who are concerned, and the passage of time lightens the burden of the pain until it is an ache and then mostly just a memory. But the spirit is scarred and nothing is ever the same as it was before. Life *does* get better; it *does* go on and there *are* moments of joy and celebration—but it's always different somehow. Nothing we say or do can change that.

What a liberating thought!! Knowing that no one expects us to work miracles frees us up to carry on our ministry without needing to know the mythical magical formula for making everything fine and dandy. We are free to concentrate our efforts and energies on sharing our concern and ourselves with the bereaved. How is this mission accomplished? Not by memorizing a list of sayings and snappy slogans, but by remembering to follow a few simple guidelines and leading with the heart, tempered by a minimal portion of common sense. The guidelines themselves are common sense, but identifying them beforehand and being aware of them as we console bereaved people will make the encounter not only easier, but much more effective. Just remember that in times of grief, all rationalization, all logic and all lofty theology is useless. There are only feelings and if we are to speak to grief, then we must speak to feelings.

Granger Westberg identifies the feelings that people experience as they move through the grief process. In his book *Good Grief*, Westberg says that in most cases, the first feeling is shock, a temporary denial process which serves as a natural anesthetic and make it possible to live with the reality of grief.

It was Sunday morning. I had made the three-hour trip back from my parents' apartment just a few hours before. My dad and I had spent the previous thirty-six hours together saying goodbye. When I left the apartment, I was fairly certain that Dad's illness was nearly over; he would be dying soon. I was teaching my Sunday school class when someone came to the door, summoning me to the telephone. It was my wife who had stayed with my folks. "Roger, your dad's gone," she said. My immediate reaction was—against all logic and reason—disbelief. Right up until that phone call, there was a part of me that believed that at the eleventh hour, the cavalry would charge in with a miracle cure; a divine magician would pull a rabbit out of a Big Hat and Dad's lung cancer would go into remission and disappear. Intellectually, I knew that there was no way that could happen. But in the grief process, intellect takes a back seat to the guts; emotions call the shots.

The worship service was due to start in forty minutes. In the meantime, I had to tell my children, ages six and three, that their grandpa had died. A retired minister in my church offered to take over the worship service for me. I considered it briefly, but felt a need to do it myself. The emotional anesthetic known as shock enabled me to do the service (although I don't remember much about it now), as well as get through the myriad of details immediately accompanying a death in the family. The shock didn't wear off until just after Dad's funeral service three days later. Rationally and intellectually, I remember many of the people and events of those three days; emotionally, I remember the numbness. In "normal grief," this shock phase is temporary, although feelings of being removed from reality may recur periodically.

Westberg says that the most common second stage of grief involves the expression of emotions. When Dad died, I was somewhat disturbed at myself for not shedding tears from the time he died until the funeral was over. After all, I loved him and "proper" expression of grief—I thought—was to cry. Was something wrong with me? Nope. After the shock wore off, I was able to cry freely. How good that felt! When I had finished crying that first time, I felt cleansed. In the time since, I have felt moved to repeat that same cleansing process, which I have come to realize is a way of externalizing our grief—a way of getting the event outside of ourselves. This externalization can take any form, from quiet sobbing to full-fledged hysterics.

I was serving as a student chaplain in a regional hospital located in a state full of mountain people. Life and death were pretty basic there. Many of the patients I saw in the hospital were knife or gunshot victims whose wounds were acquired during family feuds. Needless to say, much of the "sophistication" of my culture was absent from this lifestyle. I accompanied the doctor into the waiting room where he told a woman that, although the medical team had done all it could, her husband had died of a cardiac arrest. With a piercing scream, she threw herself on the floor and began thrashing around, her verbalizations a confused jumble of prayer, cursing and the names of her husband, God and

Jesus all mixed together. The relatives with her stood by passively, making no move to snap her out of it. I was horrified! After all, this flew in the face of what my culture had taught was proper! I looked at the doctor, fully expecting him to inject the lady with Thorazine or some other sedative. Instead, he too, stood by and let the woman express the grief she felt in a genuine and honest way.

Reflecting back on the incident, it occurs to me that this lady most probably made a quicker recovery from her grief than would someone who kept her or his feelings all bottled up. No matter how long it takes, grief will come out. The bereaved person has the choice of undergoing "good grief" now or "bad grief" later.

Depression and loneliness comprise the third stage of the grief journey. The grieving person feels as if his or her predicament is the only one of its kind in the entire course of human history. To be sure, everyone's grief journey *is* different. But the grieving person will often feel as though no other person has ever grieved; no one else has experienced the loss as profoundly as this loss. Even God seems far away. Prayers offered with all the spiritual strength one can muster don't even get past the ceiling. The sense of isolation is very strong; the person in grief often feels as if everyone and everything around him is nothing more than an illusion— a holograph without substance. The situation seems like a bad dream and yet, the bereaved person knows that the situation is very real. There will be no escape with the coming of morning's light. This knowledge engenders a sense of hopelessness, which is the stuff out of which depression is made. Depression severely impairs the will to live and the prospect of living day in and day out in this hopeless state is bleak indeed.

At about the same time, the person in grief notices a change in relationships. In the case of a death, the surviving spouse must reorient herself or himself to a single lifestyle.

For someone who has been half of a couple for years, this adjustment is considerable. Sometimes the feeling of being the "odd one out" compounds the problem of isolation. Someone else offered me this perspective: "It's a lot easier not to go out in the first place than it is to come home to an empty house."

There are often symptoms of physical distress in the grief process. A study done by Dr. Eric Lundemann demonstrated a positive correlation between grief and ulcerative colitis, a painful and sometimes dangerous condition of the large bowel. Other physical symptoms may occur in the form of headache, stomach problems, chest pains, heart palpitations and a number of other conditions. These symptoms can be treated to give temporary relief and usually disappear after awhile. However, sometimes they persist, which might indicate a case of arrested grief. I have no empirical data on this, but I do know a lady who lost her husband many years ago, but to my knowledge, she never shed a single tear. Since the time of her loss, she has had one health problem after another, some of them severe. Grief will come out.

The other initial dynamics of grief consist of panic, guilt and anger or resentment. Panic is often related to the fear of losing one's mind. Grieving people are forgetful and disoriented, which causes them to wonder if they're going crazy. Guilt is manifested in nearly every human relationship. It is a guilt which is brought on by words, thoughts or deeds against someone else. Often there is another kind of guilt which imposes the responsibility for a lot of unrealistic expectations on the part of the one grieving. An acquaintance of mine still hasn't dealt with the guilt he feels over the fact that he went to work thirty minutes before his terminally ill father died. Years later, his lifestyle reflects his unresolved guilt and its attendant self-loathing.

57

Anger can and often does come out against everyone, including God. Often, the anger is directed by the widow toward the dead spouse for dying or the doctors who failed to save him. Or in a different kind of grief situation, it can be directed toward the boss who signed the termination notice or processed the transfer orders. Let me emphasize that anger is a normal part of the grief process and should be let out freely. Unresolved anger festers and become resentment, which can cripple a person emotionally for the rest of his or her life.

This isn't a complete list of the dynamics of grief, but it is important to be aware of the initial manifestations of bereavement, for the simple reason that we can be tremendous help to grieving friends just by knowing what to expect. Familiarity with the grief process enables us to give assurances to those in grief who fear for their mental health. We can alleviate a lot of panic just by knowing that our friend is grieving normally. Once we recognize the dynamics of grief, we can begin to deal with them without fear. We can employ certain principles, guidelines and survival tactics which will help the process along. Remember that it is not our aim to eradicate grief or to make it go away before it is time. We can no more do that than we can make a flower bloom before it is ready. As care-givers, our role is to give support and encouragement to bereaved friends as they move from phase to phase until the will to live and an appreciation for life returns.

While there are very few specific things to say to people in grief, there are several things we can *do* that will render effective care. When we are placed in the role of care-giver, we can do our best work when we remember these things:

Sometimes silence says more than all the words in the world. I believe that of all things our society fears, silence has to be in the top three. We surround ourselves with noise. We have the television on, not for what's showing but for

58

background noise it provides. According to statistics, the average American home contains five radios. As we walk down the street or run through the park, we stick head sets into our ears. During worship, we celebrate communion—the one time above all others to sense the presence of God—while the organist fills up the silence. Unless we fill the air with glib conversation, we perceive person-to-person encounters to be stiff and awkward.

The Old Testament book of Ecclesiastes reminds us that, "to everything there is a season and a time for every purpose under heaven." One particular we could insert behind that admonition is, "A time to talk and a time to keep silent." A grief situation is often one of those times for silence. Grief evokes feelings that are too profound for words. In a time of loss, there isn't anything to say. No words ever replace the loss. Nothing we can say will sound like anything other than what it is—lame, banal and most of all, desperate. Silence, on the other hand is more genuine and allows for a deeper level of communication—and communion—between the care-giver and the care-needing.

As we read the Old Testament, we're most often regaled by images of fire and brimstone, earthquakes and thunder. But this is the same place where the psalmist passes along these words from the Lord: "Be still, and know that I am God" (Psalm 46:10a, NIV). It's the place where Elijah, after searching for God in all the clamor of earthquakes, wind and fire, encounters God as the Still Small Voice (cf. 1 Kings 19). If we are to be good care-givers, we must learn to be comfortable with silence. We must recognize it as a valuable thing to carry with us in our grief-therapy tool kit. We must give ourselves permission to stay silent when the occasion calls for it and let a deeper level of communication take place between us and the one who is in grief.

Don't be afraid to touch. It's interesting to me how different cultures and societies attach different meanings to the identical sets of behavior. Nowhere is this more applicable than in the case of touching. Slowly, we are starting to move away from old connotations, but in many parts of America, it's still the case that any touching other than a formal handshake implies something sexual. Actually, nothing could be further from the truth, and people in Europe, the Middle East and other areas of the world have known this and accepted it for a long time.

In the world of the grieving, human touch is especially important. It reassures the person in grief that the people he sees around him are real, not just illusions. It also gives him something or someone on which to "anchor" himself as he moves through the time of greatest pain.

Back in Chapter 2 there is an account of a man who died in what was either a hunting accident or a suicide. The encounter I had with his brother underscores the importance of touching. The brother was a real "macho man." He usually greeted with a punch on the shoulder. Yet, when I went to his house after his brother died, he virtually ran to me and threw his arms around me, hanging on for dear life. When someone is suffering from the pain caused by bereavement, then social conventions be damned!

Many times, I have gone to a home or hospital and hung on to a new widow or widower, letting them hang on to me at the same time. After the funeral and the grief process continues, I wouldn't think of casually touching those people. But when the trust level is there and grief's pain is acute, a hand on the shoulder or the arm, an embrace or a hug or even a fervent clasp of the hands has the power to bring strength and reality to the grieving, as well as convey to them your willingness to share their experience.

Grieving people need human contact! A friend of ours lost her husband nearly twenty years ago. A "people person," she had always been gregarious, outgoing and eminently sociable. After her husband died, she did everything she could to fill up her time. She took a day job at the university; in the evening she worked at the community theater, volunteering to help with every production on the schedule, always the last one to leave. And late at night, when everyone else in her town was either home or out having fun with their friends, she would go to the all-night supermarket and walk up and down the aisles, talking to anyone she could find—just for the human contact. Touching the person in grief does much to alleviate feelings of isolation. The macho types just don't make it when the little child in each of us reaches out for comfort and relief from the hurting. Bereaved people need to satisfy their tactile sense on the road to recovery.

Let the bereaved take the conversational initiative. When I go visit a family after a death has occurred, there are certain things I must find out. Since I will be in charge of the funeral service, I must know which funeral home is handling the arrangements, which day and at what hour the service will be held, whether the family would like to have the funeral dinner at the church or somewhere else, whether there are people coming in from out of town who need rides or other accommodations, and some of the vital statistics on the deceased (date of birth, cause of death and so on). Admittedly, these are questions that don't come even close to imparting strength and comfort, but they are necessary questions that must be answered so that planning can get underway. In other words, I often approach a grief situation with a mental agenda that I know must be covered by the time I leave.

At the same time, the grieving person has his own agenda with which to contend. It might consist of anything from verbally reliving every detail of the deceased's final hours to venting anger, to talking about plans that must be made, to discussing the college football team or the outcome of the World Series. Always follow the grieving person's agenda. Talk about whatever he or she wants to talk about.

If you're very close to the person in grief, the conversation will probably move quickly to the deeper issues that lie near the core of the grief. When the bereaved person is a more casual acquaintance, then it may take a little longer to move to that level. Whether you talk about deep subjects or not, however, always remember that along with silence, there is also a time to talk. You are helping the grieving person by allowing him or her to verbalize what might be on his or her mind. The key to successful interaction is to let grieving people talk about whatever they wish. Listen reflectively. Respond to the things they say, but don't monopolize the conversation; leave plenty of opportunity for them to cover whatever subjects might be on their agenda. Try to put your agenda aside, at least for the time being. Often, I will have to suspend my questions about the nuts-and-bolts for awhile until the bereaved person's agenda has been covered. Remember that you are there to meet his/her needs, not necessarily your own.

Sometimes the grieving person will want to talk about anything else except the immediate troubles at hand. The conversation may take on an air of unreality as the pall of death, a lost job, a severe illness, the prospect of moving, a divorce or something else hangs heavy in the air and the grieving person talks about the stock market or a church committee meeting or politics or any number of other things. Remember that this is okay! More than likely, the bereaved person is in a state of shock which numbs the senses and makes it impossible to live the grief's reality.

At other times, the grieving person will want to retell the story over and over again. I have sat in living rooms and heard accounts given several times verbatim, almost as if they were being read off scripts. Whatever verbal direction a

62

grieving person may be heading, the most effective thing we can do is ride along with him or her. When the silence is over, and the time to talk has come, follow the bereaved person's conversational topics. And rather than saying, "Don't talk about it now," be supportive, responsive and encouraging as events, feelings and perhaps basketball scores come up in the conversation.

"I'm sorry." Throughout the first part of this book, I have said again and again that there is no magic word which will fit every grief situation. The simple statement, "I'm sorry," comes close to being the exception to that rule. "I'm sorry," can be offered in complete sincerity no matter what the circumstances of grief happen to be. Take the case, for instance, of an elderly person's death after a long and painful illness. While that death can be considered part of the healing process, the pain of separation from that loved one is no less real. "I'm sorry," might describe your feelings about a friend's grief rather than the dead person's release from suffering. Perhaps you didn't know the person who died, but knew that person's family. Again, "I'm sorry," covers your feelings about sharing that grieving person's pain. "I'm sorry," can mean any number of things—I'm sorry she's dead; I'm sorry you feel badly; I'm sorry I feel badly—or whatever else is appropriate and sincere. As long as you have a definite meaning in mind, the words, "I'm sorry," will sound sincere to a hurting friend.

It is dangerous to think of, "I'm sorry," as a convenient catch-all phrase; however, in most grief situations, this is a conversational opener which lets the bereaved choose the direction the conversation will take. It also says you care.

Offer a remembrance. One of the things I found especially helpful when Dad died was that some people would mention a specific instance in which Dad touched their lives. People from the churches he served wrote something in the sympathy cards they sent about how Dad helped them through a particularly rough time in their lives or gave them a new insight which helped them grow spiritually or how he related so well to the youth in the church. Friends of the family told me about the fun they had had with Dad; they mentioned his sense of humor and his willingness to engage in practical jokes.

People will often avoid talking about the deceased because they're afraid that mention of their name might further upset the loved ones left behind. Remember that the person to whom you're talking is in grief and already upset. The best way to deal with the feelings of bereavement is honestly and without denial or minimization. In other words, don't refer to Aunt Minnie's terminal condition as "her little health problem."

If remembering a cherished incident from the past brings tears, remember that tears are good! Herb Miller, a wise author and minister, once said something to the effect that grief cannot be dry cleaned; it must be washed away in tears. In my experience, remembrances have been a source of comfort rather than a cause for additional grief. I think it's because, although I knew Dad was an important guy, hearing other people tell me how Dad touched their lives affirmed his importance in the bigger scheme of things.

Be careful about the remembrance you offer, though. The best kind are those that can be offered honestly, highlighting qualities such as friendliness, concern for others, commitments to justice and peace, a sense of humor and so on. A reminiscence about that lost weekend in Tijuana may not be especially comforting to a grieving family. Again, the watchwords here are honesty and sincerity. A willingness to confront grief feelings and affirm a person's importance— not only in death, but in all other grief situations as well— can do much to comfort those who are bereaved.

Make specific offers of assistance. When grief happens, everything else seems to stop. The little details that we take

64

for granted in normal times are mentally set aside as we become preoccupied with our pain. But life does indeed go on and this is where concerned friends and care-givers can be of invaluable assistance to bereaved persons. While it seems to place a burden on people when we say, "If there's anything I can do to help, let me know," we can lighten the burden dramatically when we offer to provide child care for the kids or make phone calls to individuals or see to some details that must be seen to or answer the telephone for awhile or receive visitors to the house so that the grieving person can get some rest. It's amazing how physically taxing a grief experience can be; in every way, the grieving person is left feeling drained and exhausted. The circumstances surrounding grief, as well as the process of working through details, nearly always rob the bereaved person of sleep.

Another thing you can offer to do is keep a record of the gifts of food and other forms of assistance that come in during the first few days after a death. Most people in grief aren't sure about what needs to be done and while some know what needs to be done, they are hesitant to ask for assistance. For many fiercely independent individuals, to ask for help of any kind goes against their nature. When we make specific offers of assistance, it is easier for the independent person to accept the help. They don't have to ask us because we offered. So think of anything. No offer of help is too small, for literally everything needs to be taken care of during the initial stages of grief. You can be a great help by offering to do something specific for a grieving friend.

Assure the grieving person of God's presence, if you believe in it. In the last chapter, we discussed the fact that telling someone the misfortune is "God's will" is quite dangerous. It is counterproductive to lead the grieving one to believe that God was behind a death or a divorce or the loss of a job. This is not to say, however, that any mention of God whatsoever should be avoided. On the contrary, God's presence and the allusion to it can serve as a great source of comfort and strength.

As we have seen, one of the dynamics of grief is anger and often that anger is directed at God. The grieving person will usually ask the timeless question, "Why me?" The assumption behind this question, of course, is that God caused the grief. Harold Kushner underwent a struggle of faith which he chronicled in his book *When Bad Things Happen to Good People* (Schocken Books, New York). His son Aaron contracted progeria, a condition which causes premature aging. In essence, Kushner's son died of old age when he was fourteen. An important part of Kushner's struggle through the grief process involved his effort to find a place for God in it. He experienced anger and questioned his faith for a long time before coming to the conclusion that God was present in the situation, not as the cause of the disease, but as the source of the family's survival as they dealt with that death.

God allows us to feel grief, although he does not cause it. The third chapter of the Old Testament book of Lamentations makes it clear that although he has put grief into our emotional repertoire, God never willingly inflicts grief on us. To feel as though God has abandoned us in times of grief is normal and natural. The writer of the gospel tells us that Jesus Christ, at his greatest moment of pain on the cross, uttered that cry of despair, "My God, my God, why have you forsaken me?" (Mark 15:34). When the bereaved persons feel this same desperation, it is entirely appropriate to remind them that God is indeed present and will make it possible to survive and recover. Try to avoid sounding preachy or Pollyanna-ish as you do this. Similarly, don't mention it if you have doubts about God's existence yourself. That sounds rather self-evident, but I have heard some professed agnostics talk about God's presence to hurting friends because they thought that was what they wanted to hear. The result sounded insincere and was thus counter-productive.

If you believe in God, share your sense of God's presence. If some verses of scripture have touched you in a special way during your own grief journey, share them. Some that meant a lot to me in my own moments of pain include a section from Paul's letter to the Romans:

Who shall separate us from the love of Christ? Shall trouble or hardship or persecution or famine or nakedness or danger or sword? As it is written: "For your sake we face death all day long; we are considered as sheep to be slaughtered." No, in all these things we are more than conquerors through him who loved us. For I am convinced that neither death nor life, neither angels nor demons, neither the present nor the future, nor any powers, neither height nor depth, nor anything else in all creation, will be able to separate us from the love of God that is in Christ Jesus or Lord (Romans 8:35-39 NIV).

I especially like this passage from Isaiah:

Fear not, for I am with you; be not dismayed, for I am your God. I will strengthen you, I will help you, I will uphold you with the right hand of my righteousness . . . for I am the Lord your God, who takes hold of your right hand and says to you, Do not fear; I will help you (Isaiah 41:10, 13).

There are others in Isaiah that are equally comforting. Here is a bit of encouragement from the book of Joshua:

Have I not commanded you? Be strong and courageous. Do not be terrified; do not be discouraged,

for the Lord your God will be with you wherever
you go (Joshua 1:9).

And of course, the perennial favorite, Psalm 23:

The Lord is my Shepherd; I shall not want. He
makes me to lie down in green pastures, he leads me
beside still waters, he restores my soul. He leads me
in the paths of righteousness for his name's sake.
Even though I walk through the valley of the
shadow of death, I fear no evil, for thou art with me.
Thy rod and thy staff they comfort me. Thou pre-
parest a table before me in the presence of my enemies.
Thou anointest my head with oil, my cup overflows.
Surely goodness and mercy shall follow me all the
days of my life and I shall dwell in the house of the
Lord forever.

In one of Jesus' last discourses with his disciples before
his arrest, he assured them that he would not leave them
comfortless, but would send a spirit of comfort and strength
to get the disciples through the worst of times (cf. John 14).
That promise can become ours in our times of emotional
pain and suffering. We can remind those we serve of that
promise as encouragement in their own situations.

God is indeed present in every grief situation. He is
present through the people who gather around to give care,
through the promises that have been recorded in scripture,
as the "still small voice," which resides in each person. A
reminder to the grieving that they need not undergo this
experience totally alone can be of great help, if you—and
they—believe in this sincerely.

A popular prose-poem tells the story of a man who had
a dream; he saw two sets of footprints on the sand of a
beach. One set was his, the other God's. He followed the

68

footprints and saw the events of his life along the way. As they passed the painful times, he noticed that only one set of footprints could be seen. He asked God why God had deserted him when he'd needed him most. His answer was that the footprints belonged to God, who had carried the man over the rough times.

Allow for the full range of feelings and emotions.
Ultimately, people react to grief in their own individualized ways. While there are dynamics common to nearly every grief situation, there's no way to tell just which dynamic a person will experience at any given time. For some, the first expression of emotion will take the form of tears. For others, it will be anger. Whatever emotions happen to be on the surface, the best thing care-givers can do at any time is to encourage the ventilation of those feelings. Sometimes this may not be so pleasant to the ones giving the care. It's uncomfortable enough for most of us to be in the presence of someone else crying; occasionally those in grief will vent their anger by cursing and using vulgarities. Our sensibilities may be assaulted as we hear words we were taught never to use, at least in polite company. If this happens, remember that what you're seeing is pure, unadulterated pain brought on by the sense of the loss of someone or something very important. This is pain that must come out, either now or later. Better it should come out now! The sooner that pain is externalized, the sooner the grieving person can get on with the business of recovery. In other words, this is not the time for corrective lectures to the bereaved on social propriety. We can help best when we make every effort to be non-judgmental in our response to such intense negative expressions of emotion.

On the other hand, I have seen grieving people who really wanted to laugh at some incidental thing, but were stifled by those around them who were conditioned to believe that there is no room in grief for laughter. Believe

69

me, there is! If something strikes the grieving person as funny, feel free to allow them to laugh—and feel free to laugh with that person if you feel so moved. Besides being a release from tension, laughter has other healing properties.

Norman Cousins contracted a degenerative spinal condition. Doctors gave him one chance in five hundred for a recovery from this painful disease which would eventually take his life. Cousins refused to accept that prognosis and embarked upon a search for other treatments. In his quest for relief from pain, Cousins took massive doses of vitamin C and discovered the medicine of laughter. Watching Marx Brothers movies and film clips of old "Candid Camera" shows, he found that ten minutes of deep belly-laughter provided him with two hours of painfree sleep. Tests taken before and after laughter showed a positive drop in Cousins' red blood cell sedimentation rate, a key diagnostic measure. Norman Cousins eventually entered a state of full recovery and credits this miracle to laughter, his will to live and the doctors' willingness to try an unusual treatment protocol. The full account of Norman Cousins' experience with laughter may be found in his book *Anatomy of an Illness As Perceived by the Patient.*

The phone rang on a Monday night. It was the father of my wife's best friend, who told us that his son-in-law had just died of Hodgkin's disease. He was 31. We made immediate plans to go be with Karen.

The reality of the situation didn't hit me until I saw Elwin lying in the casket. The ravages of both his disease and the chemotherapy treatments had exacted a terrible toll on him; the tragedy of life cut short impressed itself upon us in an indelible way.

As we sat with Karen, looking at the flowers around the casket, she remarked about how the arrangements at the top looked like a Christmas tree. The image of a Christmas tree juxtaposed into the viewing room of a funeral home occurred to all of us at once and our laughter reverberated around the entire facility. The laughter was right and good. Rather than desecrating Elwin's memory, we anointed it with our laughter, which was a genuine emotional expression and ultimately a catalyst to Karen's recovery.

Allow for the full range of emotions, from belly-laughter to soul-deep rage. Don't try to censor the language of grief; instead, serve as a sounding board, listening reflectively and non-judgmentally. Listen with empathy. Give the grieving person permission—whether verbally or nonverbally—to be herself. This way, the journey through grief can be made with all possible dispatch.

Make use of prayer. Prayer is a powerful thing. From the earliest eras of human history, people have recognized the potential for achieving communication with the Supreme Being. Jesus made extensive use of prayer and urged others to do the same.

But much of prayer's potential is wasted, simply because people are afraid to pray. They feel intimidated because their prayers don't come out sounding like the prayers of all the ministers they've heard. They're uncomfortable with King James English—the thees, thous, whithers and goeths—and they have never cultivated a stained-glass voice. Consequently, people tend to feel that not only will they sound stupid, but their prayers will be ineffective as well. People seem to labor under the delusion that God listens only to the prayers of the professionals. Consequently, in most grief situations, prayer is one of those things that is relegated to a cubbyhole somewhere in the process, say, for instance, at the conclusion of the pastor's visit or during the funeral and burial services.

Maybe this sounds like a generalization to you. Maybe you can think of several instances in your own experience when a prayer shared by a friend filled you with a sense of assurance that whatever had happened to you was indeed survivable. Maybe you already know that God hears every prayer that's offered up, regardless of the credentials you might hold. Maybe you realize that the prayer given in conversational American can be just as effective as the ones in King James English and sometimes effective prayers take the form not of words, but of "sighs too deep for words."

In my own life, the most powerful and effective prayers that I have shared have come from people who were not professional clergy, but committed laypeople with a sensitivity to the presence of God in human activity. Whether it was during a grief situation or at the communion table on Sunday morning during worship, many prayers offered by laypeople touched a responsive chord in my own spirit and made me able to partake of the strength and power that God has to give.

In a vast majority of cases, grieving people need and appreciate someone who offers to pray with them. There are times when the pain of grief preoccupies us to the point that we cannot pray ourselves, even though we feel the need for prayer.

I remember experiencing this phenomena at least twice; the first time being when Dad lay dying. Near the end of our last visit together, he asked me to have a prayer with him. I thought he wanted me to step out of the role of grieving son and into the role of the pastoral care-giver. Now, years later, I realize that he would have made the same request of any one of his loved ones, whether or not they were professional clergy. At any rate, when he asked me to pray with him, I found myself floundering about for things to say. Imagine that: me, a cleric, accustomed to praying before large groups of people right off the top of my head and the bottom of my heart; a public speaker never before left speechless—at a total loss for a prayer. I finally did get one out, but it was so difficult; probably one of the hardest things I've ever had to do.

The second time that happened was the morning my son Seth went to surgery to have his eye repaired. As I saw him looking so small under his surgical bonnet with his left eye patched, an I-V running into his arm, sedated and without his normal bright inquisitiveness—I needed a prayer so badly! Everyone around me—family and friends—assumed that I, as the minister, could take care of that for myself; in fact, nothing could have been further from the truth.

The point is that when it comes to prayer, you can be most effective by not assuming anything. Don't assume that the minister will handle all of the need for prayer in the situation. Don't assume that your prayers are too clumsy to be helpful. Don't assume that you will be branded a religious fanatic if you offer to pray in the presence of grief. Don't assume that if a grieving person doesn't ask for or mention prayer that he or she doesn't feel the need for it. If you have the conviction and courage to do so, offer to share a prayer with those in grief. Most of the time, they will accept your offer gratefully and the words you say will have less effect in the long run than the fact that you cared enough to risk offering this powerful medicine for the hurting spirit.

Now, there may be a time when you offer a prayer and the person in grief says, "No!" That's okay, too. Remember that one of the dynamics of grief is anger and often the anger is directed at God. Sometimes the person in the initial stages of grief is so angry at God that he feels no desire to have any contact whatsoever with the Almighty. I think that God is certainly prepared to handle any anger we might direct toward him; like the father whose child is caught up in the throes of a tantrum, God continues to love us and hold us until the anger subsides. Whatever else, don't feel that you are being rejected as a care-giver or a friend just because the person doesn't accept your offer of prayer. At least you gave the bereaved person a choice in the matter.

Also, don't assume that because a person turns down an offer to pray that he or she will never want you to make that offer again. In time, with good nurturing through the grief recovery process, the anger will subside and the grieving person may feel the need and the desire to talk to God in prayer. Just remain open to any possibilities and regard each visit you make as a unique and individual moment without basing it on previous visits. That way prayer—and your willingness to offer it—will be available whenever it's needed.

One thing we often overlook is the fact that prayer is a form of conversation with God. We who have the prayer item on our agenda think that we are the ones who have to do all the talking. Quite to the contrary! Often, the offer of prayer brings forth prayer from the grieving one. A pastor friend of mine says, "I think it's helpful to ask the bereaved to pray, instead of me or someone else doing it all the time. It's okay if it's a silent prayer, too. This shows confidence in the person and gives the person permission to tell God all about it."

I'll never forget the first time I was jolted off my "prayer agenda." I was visiting a man who had just found out that he had cancer—major cancer. We talked a long time about the implications of that and he was able to express many different feelings, from anger to hope. As I prepared to leave, I offered to pray with him. He accepted the offer and I gave a prayer for strength, encouragement, alleviation of pain and eventual healing in any of its forms. I said, "Amen," and assumed that that was it, but my friend then began to pray, himself. It was a beautiful prayer from the heart. Your prayers often give the grieving permission to pray, where they may have previously felt none. And that is one of the very best things you can ever do for those who experience grief.

Time is healing. Until I went through it myself, I had heard this said and always thought it was a cliché, offered in the absence of anything else meaningful to say. From this perspective, I can see that it is indeed true, no matter how trite it may sound. The only way a surgical wound can heal is with time. The only way a bone knits after a fracture is with time. The only way measles or mumps (not to mention the common cold) go away is with time. And the only way grief is replaced by an affirmation of life is with time.

If the grief proceeds as it should and if concerned persons give the kind of care that enables the bereaved person to feel "good grief," then there will come a day when the grieving person won't feel the sharp sting of inner pain quite so acutely. Gradually, the sting will diminish until it is mostly gone. That can't happen before it's time though.

The way most grief processes work is like this: At first, there are many bad days. Then, for one day maybe, there is a good day. Then more bad days and then two or three good days. Then a shorter string of bad days, then several good ones in a row. Gradually, the good days outnumber the bad ones and life returns to a semblance of normalcy. This is not to say that things will be the same as they were, but life will become better.

Only someone who has been through a major recovery from grief can make the assertion that time heals. Even then, it is very difficult for the grieving person to internalize that assurance. The person in grief may hear the care-giver say it; she may know intellectually that it's true. She may have said it herself to someone else. But at the time of grief's greatest pain, there is little, if any, chance that the grieving person will believe that information emotionally. This does not mean that you should not offer it as a word of encouragement; it means that whoever offers it should not be surprised or upset if the recipient does not readily believe it.

When this happens, what do you do? Keep caring; remain available to the one in grief. Continue to do the things you're doing to aid in the grief recovery process, in the belief that time *does* heal wounds. Your perseverance will pay off in great dividends to the bereaved far into the future.

* * * * * * *

These principles of care-giving can and should be used in virtually every grief situation. When they are, the care-giver can approach the grief situation with confidence, knowing that his or her caring, translated into action, helped the grief-stricken friend or family member celebrate life once again.

5

Some Examples

In Chapter 1, we noted the fact that grief can be caused by any number of different events: death, illness, loss of a home, a child moving away or the adjustment to a new lifestyle—all can precipitate a grief reaction. In all of these situations, however, the same basic principles of care-giving outlined in the preceding chapters, plus the gift of presence highlighted in Chapter 2, can be applied with great effectiveness.

Consider, for instance, the case of Tom, a man in his late sixties. Tom had lost both his legs through amputation and was due to be transferred from the hospital to a nursing home. This meant that he would be losing his own home and all that goes with it; privacy, control over his own life and so on.

Mary, his care-giver during this particular visit, was a woman of strong faith who believed in the power of prayer.

She did not hesitate to use this prayer to impart strength and a measure of hope to Tom. The visit went like this:

> *Mary:* Hello, Tom; I hear you're leaving.
> *Tom:* Yes, I'm leaving for the nursing home.
> *Mary:* I'm so sorry I didn't have some good visits with you, but it seemed that there was always something to keep us from getting together: therapy, thermometers, meals coming in, nurses, naps . . .
> *Tom:* Yes, we didn't have much luck, did we? (pause) While I think about it, will you get my wallet and things out of the top drawer?

Mary did this and helped Tom get his personal effects in order for the trip to the nursing home. Then she asked, "How do you feel about going?"

> *Tom:* I don't feel very good.
> *Mary:* You've been discouraged, haven't you?
> *Tom:* Yes.
> *Mary:* Are you fearful of the future, what it may hold?
> *Tom:* Yes, I'm fearful, I dread it.
> *Mary:* You're afraid that things won't go well?
> *Tom:* Yes.
> *Mary:* You're going where you will be able to get the care that you need. (long pause) You do have a half-brother, don't you?
> *Tom:* I have two.
> *Mary:* Well, good. Maybe you'll see them once in awhile. (pause) Do you belong to a church? Do you have a minister?

Tom replied that he had never gone to church and consequently didn't have a minister of his own. Mary told Tom he didn't have to wait until he joined a church to start talking to God. She told Tom how she prayed often and in prayer found some strength and encouragement. She offered to pray for him. Tom surprised her pleasantly by asserting, "And that's the best thing you can do for me!" Mary continued to tell Tom about the advantages of prayer and then she made a minor gaffe. She said, "You know, you're still young yet. You have a lot of good years." Remember that this was one of the sayings we felt was best to avoid. While Mary was trying to tell Tom that he could still have a full and useful life, Tom may have interpreted it as a sentence to hard time. Being as depressed as he was, maybe he didn't *want* a lot more years!

The visit went on in a somewhat lighter vein, talking about Tom's and Mary's ages and comparing hobbies. His social worker came into the room and cut the visit short. However, we can see several things that were both helpful and not especially helpful.

Mary made good use of leading questions to draw out into the open Tom's feelings about leaving. Once she got him talking, it seemed that he was able to say, at least, "I'm scared." Her questions about the brothers, church and minister and the comment about his going where he can get the care he needed may have looked on the surface as though Mary was trying to play "fix-it" (a no-no), but I believe her intention was to find out what resources he had around him and point out to him that he wouldn't be totally alone. The best part of the visit seemed to be when Mary awakened in Tom the realization that he, too, could pray and draw upon God as a source of strength. We cannot know if Tom ever followed up on this, but at least, for the moment, his situation looked a little less bleak.

Later, Mary told me that this was a time when she wished she could follow this patient "out of the hospital" and into the nursing home, just to see how he got along. She was very available to this man and seemed to be willing to continue to give what emotional and spiritual support she could through her own use of prayer. Meanwhile, she stayed in contact with the hospital social worker so that she could keep in touch with Tom as he left the hospital.

Sometimes, we are thrust into the role of care-giver before we realize what's happening. One day I was making the rounds in my role of chaplain in a regional hospital when I happened upon a lady whom I had not seen before.

Me: I'm Rev. Miller, one of the chaplains here in the hospital. I noticed you got in recently; is that right?

Helen: Wednesday. I came in Wednesday.

This surprised me, for I had not seen her before and this was Saturday. She explained that she had been in the heart unit since Wednesday. Then, without any prompting on my part, she added, "I lost my dear husband. That's why I'm here with this sickness." Her face clouded up to cry.

"I see," I said. "Did your husband pass away recently?" I thought that maybe the fellow died six months or a year ago. Helen knocked me over when she answered, "Wednesday." I checked to see if I had heard her correctly. I had.

Helen: Yes, he died in the ambulance. I was in the ambulance with him when he died and they just brought me in. That's when I had my heart attack.

I answered her, "I'm so very sorry for your trouble and for your sadness. It must be a terrible feeling to lose a loved one so suddenly like that."

80

Helen: Yes, it is. (pause) I have sixteen living children.

She said this as if it were something to hang onto and indicated that she would be depending on them. I asked if there was anything I could do for her at the moment (see, even I have said things that have only dubious, if not downright detrimental value! That wasn't the last time I ever said that, either.). She told me that she would appreciate a prayer, so, taking her hand, I said something like, "Our Heavenly Father, we come to you in this time of grief, casting ourselves before you; trusting that you will provide us strength to face the difficult days ahead. Be with Helen's family and help them to experience the love and support that at times like this, comes only from you. These things we pray, in the name of the Father, the Son and the Holy Spirit. Amen."

Following the prayer, she asked me to come back and see her again, which I took as a sort of dismissal. Now, years later, I'm not so sure. I walked out of the room shaken because what I had intended to be a routine initial patient visit turned quickly to a grief call, as quickly as acid turns litmus paper. In the days that followed this visit, I saw her again and again, talking with her—or rather listening to her—as she ventilated her feelings in these initial stages of her grief. Her grief was complicated by the fact that her health prevented her from attending her husband's funeral, which in nearly every case, is an important part of the grieving process. Funeral services afford the bereaved a sense of closure on the particular phase of the death experience. To miss a funeral service for a loved one, or not to have a service at all, often leaves a sense of "unfinished business" about the whole thing and in many cases retards the recovery from grief.

Sometimes grief takes different forms. I visited a member of one of my former congregations whose wife had died several months previously. He was in the hospital with a complaint of gall bladder trouble, but as I listened to him I could tell that he hurt worse from the things that he had lost than he did from the gallstones.

Harry was ninety and in great health, generally (two years earlier he had helped move the sofa into our house!). As I entered his room, I saw no cards, flowers or other expressions of concern. I had heard about his hospitalization through "the grapevine." When I came in Harry was lying on his back, staring at the ceiling. This is how the visit went:

Me: Harry?

Harry: Well, look who's here; look who's playing sick. Someone has to play sick; people do it all the time, so I thought I'd play sick this time.

Me: What are you doing in a place like this?

Harry: Oh, I'm not sick, I'm not sick; it's this little pipsqueak of a doctor that I have, you know, they have to have someone in these beds all the time to make any money in these places and I thought he'd just see me and give me something for this pain I had. You see, Saturday I was down in Mayville scouting around as I usually do and I went over to Jack Whitely's, you know them? We helped raise him when he was a youngster. Anyway, Saturday I was over to their house and they fed me a piece of watermelon. I like watermelon and they gave me some to take home with me. So I took it home and ate some more and it was all right. Then Sunday I found myself a little short of food, so I'd heard about this place down by Long Ridge that makes up sandwiches and gives them away. So I went down there and got me a couple of sandwiches and took them home and ate them and finished up the watermelon. But somehow, the rest of the watermelon was bad. Sunday night I started to feelin' bad and I tried to go to bed, but this pain just kept coming up again and again. I hurt like fire. It just felt like it was coming up the sides of my belly and grabbing me right here. So Monday I went up to see the doctor. I won't usually see one but it had been awhile since I had been looked at, so I decided to let the little fellow take a look at me to see what might be the matter. Well, he took a look here and a look there and said he couldn't find the cause of it and that he'd like me to come into the hospital to take a closer look. Now, you tell me if you know any 90-year-old man who doesn't have something wrong with him. I told him I'd take some medicine, but he insisted that I come in and I'm the kind of fellow that does just what he's told, so here I am. And they've worked me over good. I've had every X-ray they can give you and they've got about a gallon of my blood. And they're trying to put more meat on me than I've ever had before. I'm not used to eating this much. Jessie (his late wife) always cooked enough for two meals for me; I was used to eating leftovers for supper.

Me: Well, they're taking pretty good care of you, aren't they, Harry?

Harry: Oh, yes, yes; but I believe I'm going home Saturday.

Me: What makes you think so?

Harry: Well, they told this fellow that he'd be going home tomorrow. Today they told me that, so I suspect I'll go home Saturday.

Me: How do you like your new place, Harry?

Harry: (looking as if he's about to cry) Oh, not well at all, not well at all. I'm not used to living away from Mayville and the place is so small. . . .

Me: Do you have much company?

Harry: No . . . but I'm not around there much. I'm usually somewhere doing some visiting.

Me: Have you had much company here?

Harry: Robert [his son] was up once and another preacher was here, but I didn't have any use for him.

Me: Well, if you're going to be here awhile longer, I'll be stopping back to see you.

Harry: Oh, that's not necessary; I know you're busy.

Me: Not too busy to see you, Harry. Is there anything I can do for you or get for you?

Harry said that there wasn't except for a prayer. I prayed with him; he thanked me and then asked me if there was anything I remembered about the bed he was in. I said no.

Harry: This was the bed that Jessie died in. I saw it was empty as I came down the hall, so I asked for it. I was standing right where you are when the life went out of her. Robert was over there and someone else was over here. Jessie said something to the effect that she had to vomit and Robert was getting her a pan so she could accomplish that, when all of a sudden she sat straight up and looked around like this (he opened his eyes wide) and then it was just like you switched off that light over there.

Shortly after that, I concluded the visit, assuring Harry that I would be seeing him often. He seemed grateful for that. Harry's story was interesting—and infuriating. Two days after his wife died, Harry learned that she had secretly made out a will leaving everything she owned to their only child, the Robert mentioned above. The only thing that Harry was to receive was half the value of the household furniture after a sale. Of course, in order to get that money, the house and everything in it had to be sold. So here was a man who lost not only his wife of 67 years, but also with a sense of trust that Harry had for his wife all the years they had been married. In short, he felt betrayed and rightfully so.

One week after she died, Robert sold the house Harry was living in literally right out from underneath him. He repeatedly tried to find his own living quarters all around the town we lived in but the son and his wife would veto every proposal as soon as they heard about it. He wound up in an upper-floor apartment that was cold, both literally and figuratively, all by himself, in a town eight miles away from his home.

If ever a man deserved to grieve, it was Harry. And in the absence of anything to say that would "make it all better," the only thing I could do was to let him talk (he liked to do that) and cry. Eventually, Harry was able to recover from his grief and although some of the light has gone out of his eyes, I'm told that he's still active as he approaches his hundredth year. Even though I had heard most of what Harry told me before at one time or another, I felt that he needed to talk about it. Consequently, I realize the value of silence—and the gift of presence.

As we noted before, grief can happen for a number of reasons. In Harry's case, it was the death of his wife, coupled with the loss of his house and his former way of life.

In the case of Katherine, it was the impending "loss" of her son as he left for two years of service in the Army. She was in a hospital at the time and her doctors had promised her that she could be discharged in time to see him off. On the particular day I saw her, she had just been told that she would have to stay another two or three days. This, of course, would keep her from seeing her son before he left for Germany. Her son would be in Germany a very long time and with the realization that she would not be able to say goodbye properly came a deep depression.

In visiting with Katherine, I found that I could do very little as far as making anything happen the way she wanted it. As we talked, I sensed the dynamic of loneliness in Katherine and the lesson I received from that visit was that, again, it is helpful to be a listener, to give grieving people permission to cry and ventilate their feelings. This was when I first learned that care-givers are not expected to fix everything.

Katherine's story had a rather positive ending. As it turned out, her doctor changed his mind and discharged her the day after we visited, so that she was able to spend time with her son before he left. Certainly, that didn't come about through any of my influence; for the moment, I was able to be a safety valve—a sounding board—so that the grief she was feeling had a means of escape.

Grief can come on the heels of a feeling of abandonment. I remember a fellow I saw in the hospital who was dying of cancer; any terminal disease can precipitate a grief process and his grief was working itself out by producing feelings of abandonment. When I saw Carl this particular day, I asked him how he was feeling. He replied that since the night before he had hurt very, very badly, to the point that he couldn't get any rest. The conversation went on from there.

Me: Do they give you something for the pain?
Carl: Yes, they do, but it's so weak that it doesn't
     work. I ask them for another one and they

ignore me until I ask again and again. Last night I couldn't sleep until I crawled down to that end of the bed and stayed on my hand and knees. Then I got some sleep.

Me: I see. Did you ask the doctors for something stronger?

Carl: Yeah, but they haven't given me anything else. I think they've given up on me.

Me: What makes you think that?

Carl: Well, they don't work on me like they used to. It seems like they ignore me more. I think that they're just waiting for me to die.

Me: Have you talked to your doctors about this? Did you tell them what you just told me?

Carl: Aw, the doctors, they don't care. It's just like working in a slaughterhouse. You watch the beef walk through as they cut their throats and they walk on down the line while they bleed to death. At first it bothers you, but after awhile you get used to it.

Me: Is that what you feel like, a piece of beef? What would you like them to do, Carl?

Carl: Just make me better so I could go home and talk to some people. There's some people I feel like I need to talk to.

Me: Why?

Carl: To help them, because when I help them I feel better. But this, this is no life. I'd rather have six months to live where I could be comfortable and be of some good to somebody than to lie around for ten years.

We talked about his religious resources and he indicated that he did have a strong belief in God. Indeed, his faith was the one thing that was keeping him from totally giving up in despair.

I asked him if there was anything I could do for him and he said that he would like a prayer. Upon saying that, he grabbed my hand and for the first time—and one of the few subsequent times in my experience—he started praying before I did. Following the prayer, Carl was moved to cry and we talked about how it's perfectly all right to do that. Finally, Carl got tired and indicated that it would be okay for me to leave.

Carl's grieving process worked itself out in anger (remember what he said about the doctors?), loneliness, a feeling of being ignored and a desire to get back to friends whom he missed. Once again, all I did was let him get some of that anger out and cry a little bit.

A couple of years ago, I had an enlightening experience with a man who had a marginal connection to the church I presently serve. He had cancer, which was complicated by uncontrolled diabetes. His dying was long and painful. As I visited with him over a period of months, our relationship grew to the point where he trusted me with some of his deepest feelings about how it felt to lose the capacity to live. In this visit, I learned the value of silence and I found out what it's like to have my services refused.

Jim was looking exhausted when I entered his room one evening. He told me that he was discouraged; his illness had dragged on long enough. He wondered what the weather was like, all the while acting as though he were very uncomfortable. I asked him if that were true and he said that he was indeed in a lot of pain. We talked about feelings of hopelessness and being scared and he got a little agitated; I began to sense that I was heading into conversational waters in which he didn't care to be. Once this dawned on me, I told him, "Jim, don't feel as if you have to keep talking just because I'm here (he had initiated most of the conversational exchanges); you rest a little bit and I'll just sit here with you."

He acknowledged that that would be good and we sat together in silence for about ten minutes. It was a good opportunity to experience the feeling of being in a comfortable presence without speaking or filling up the air with noise. Later, his wife told me that he had remarked about how helpful that particular visit had been, although I wasn't sure at the time.

When the silence was over, Jim asked me to share some scripture passages with him, which I did. Then I told him that I had brought communion, if he wanted it. He said, "Oh, I don't know . . . I'm hurting pretty bad right now. Maybe not now." I was taken aback for just a moment, but then offered to bring it with me when I came to see him again. He told me he would appreciate that and then asked me to pray with him. Following the prayer, Jim wisely and honestly dismissed me by saying, "I'm tired now and I hurt." I told him that our church family was pulling for him and concluded the visit. I felt that this was a pivotal visit, not only for Jim who indicated later that he had received some benefit from it, but also for me. I came away with some substantial experience with the value of silence and brutally honest patients who didn't worry about my feelings.

Our pastoral relationship grew into a real friendship during the last months of Jim's life, and my association with him was truly an enriching one.

Every grief situation is unique to the person in grief and even though grief work is a big part of my profession, there are still times that I must do the best I can, feeling very inadequate when faced with the task. I present these examples to show you that you, too, can be helpful without knowing or saying any one magical formula. The things I said and did when relating to bereaved people are things that anybody could do, if they are called upon to give care.

A couple of years ago, I took another unit of Clinical Pastoral Education, a program of intensive training in relating to people who struggle with grief and other fundamental issues of life. One of my section mates was a minister who had great insights and a genuine ability to cut through smokescreens to get to the heart of any problem. He was a quiet man and a gentle man. This was enough to earn him the ironic nickname of Mad Dog.

One day he visited a patient who was in the hospital for operations on her feet, but developed "stomach pains" while she was there. During the course of this particular visit, Mad Dog discovered that the patient was the widow of a minister who had died thirteen years earlier. As it turned out, this woman still struggled with lots of grief. During the visit, she voiced some questions she never felt comfortable about asking before. Here's what I mean:

Clara: My husband was a minister. He was a good man and a good minister. We worked together in several churches. I helped him much of the time and even wrote poetry for him to use in sermons. Did you know that I write poetry?

Mad Dog: No, I wasn't aware of that.

Clara: I have received two State of Iowa literary certificates for my poetry. Would you like to hear some?

Mad Dog: Well, yes and congratulations. I would like to hear some of your writing.

She quoted her poetry and thereafter, stuck one into the conversation every now and then.

Mad Dog: Most of your poetry is religious.

Clara: Well, why shouldn't it be? I wrote poetry for my husband and for church meetings and groups. Since church and God were so important, I wrote what I felt.

Mad Dog: Do you still write poetry?

Clara: No, I haven't written for some time. Most of my poetry was written before my husband died.

Mad Dog: You have written some since he died?

Clara: Yes, but I haven't felt as much like it. I loved my husband. I don't know why he had to leave me alone.

Mad Dog: Would you like to tell me something about him?

Clara: He was a good minister, never sick in his life. We were in several churches; we were happy. Then he got lupus—some kind of tuberculosis. He died when he was only 49. That's been thirteen years now. We had two girls. One of my daughters died early in life and our other daughter lives in Paxton. Why did they leave me alone?

Mad Dog: You feel as if they left you to take care of everything by yourself. Does it seem that he chose to die and leave you?

Clara: No, I know he wouldn't do that. I know he had lupus and didn't have any choice about living. But why did he have to die so young? I should have been the one. I've been sick so much of my life. Ever since I was a little girl I've had so much wrong with me.

Mad Dog: You have suffered a great deal and you would just as soon not suffer anymore, is that it?

Clara: Yes. In February, I took an overdose of pills. It was somewhat accidental. But I wish I had gone then.

Mad Dog: And now?

Clara: Well, here I am suffering some more. You're a minister; why does God allow this suffering? Someone said to me once, "Christians suffer more than others because of Satan." What do you think? Why?

What a position in which Mad Dog should be placed! After just meeting the woman, not really knowing all that much about her theological perspective, she's asking him for concrete answers to the deepest questions of her life! Mad Dog handled it adroitly and correctly:

Mad Dog: Do you have some answers about that? What would your husband have said?

Clara: He would have said that much suffering is because of sin, but that Jesus never leaves us, no matter how hard it is.

Mad Dog: Do you feel that way?

Clara: I don't have as much faith anymore. I don't feel like I'm doing much good.

Mad Dog: Clara, there are lots of reasons that people give for suffering, but they don't always help a great deal when *we're* suffering. I do know that Jesus promised never to leave us or forsake us. I do know that he loves you and me. I also know that while you are suffering here tonight, your poetry has been very helpful and encouraging to me. Physically, I don't feel so well today, but your poetry has been very good for me.

Shortly after that, Mad Dog's visit to Clara ended with a scripture reading and a prayer of encouragement. Both participants said the conversation was helpful. For our purposes, this particular conversation has a lot to show us about the dynamics of grief. Keeping her feelings stifled for so many years, Clara seemed to be looking for someone with whom she could share the things that were going on inside her. Because she had virtually given up writing poetry, we sense some of the depression that grief brings with it. Her questions about "Why?" are certainly a part of the grieving process and in her complaint that her husband and daughter left her alone, we sense a little of the anger that is also a grief dynamic. Her suicide attempt may have been a genuine desire to discontinue living on this earth or it could have been a gesture, reaching out for someone to listen to her in a nonjudgmental way.

Mad Dog did just that. He didn't offer any bromides about cause and effect. Neither did he attempt to "fix it" and make it all better. He was wise enough to know that grief that has festered for this many years isn't dissipated in a single fifteen-minute visit. The religious conversation that he offered to Clara was not academic theologizing, but sharing of his own journey in faith, indicating to Clara a willingness to join with her in her grief. He further indicated this by sharing the fact that he didn't feel particularly well at this time and her poetry helped make him feel better. Mad Dog told me that he planned to see this woman several times during her stay in the hospital to begin working in depth on her grief recovery and as time went on, that's the way it worked out. Clara spent time in the hospital getting the bunions on her feet removed and the boils on her spirit lanced.

Perhaps you noticed that these conversations contained no magic words or special formulae; no mystical chants were offered. And yet, all of these visits were very effective to the victims of grief. Why? Because they contained the ingredients of successful grief therapy: sensitive listening, a willingness to be vulnerable, a non-judgmental attitude toward the one speaking, selectivity about what was said and most of all, a willingness to share the gift of presence.

I suspect that what you've read in these pages is nothing much more than what you've already done when your loved ones were in grief. But somehow, it's reassuring to know that when we're cast in the role of care-giver (sometimes unwillingly), there are others who share that task and that we have been given, for the most part, a sense of what to do and say that will see us through most any situation of grief.

All the books in the world, however, won't take the place or supplant the value of actual life experience. There is a world of difference between knowing how to hit a golf ball straight and true and actually doing it. Just so with grief work. I hope that this book has enabled you to give yourself permission to go out and try to give good care to those who are bereaved. You *can* do it, you know!

Afterword

No better parting words could be passed along than those that are found in the following article. It was written by N. Suzanne Miller, who happens to be my mother, and was first published in *The Disciple* magazine on November 1, 1981. The article is reprinted here by permission of both the author and the publisher.

Please Understand

by N. Suzanne Miller

Six weeks ago, my husband died. Even as I write these words, I look at them in disbelief. Bob didn't "cross over," he didn't "graduate," he died. There—it's down in black and white—his body died and I became a member of the community of the bereaved.

Basically, I know that he is alive—more alive than when he was here on earth—but his body died.

And that's when I became a member of the Community and as a member of that Community, I ask for your understanding. Not your pity, but your understanding.

Please understand that we need you—as individuals. Don't worry about saying the "right thing"—we're tired of clichés. We know our "dear one is at peace with God," and feels "no more pain," but we still miss the physical presence, the knowledge that there is one person on earth to whom we are most important; one person who knows us so completely that no words are necessary.

If we seem distant, please understand. Some of us are still in shock. Even if the illness is long and the prognosis is unfavorable, we kept the hope that death really wouldn't come. We had to do this, in order to face each hour and help give our loved ones courage.

If we seem angry, please understand. Most of us *are* angry, but we know God accepts our anger and is refining it into an energy that will be vital in our outreach to others.

If tears come at inappropriate times and places, please understand. Our emotions, even after a period of time, are still raw. We may think we are in control, but a song, or a scent, or a feeling of utter desolation may overcome us. Please accept this when it happens. Do not fuss over us or ignore us; just accept.

Conversely, if we laugh, know that deep inside we are hurting, but we know that God has given us the gift of the sense of humor and our loved one is rejoicing that we are appreciating this gift.

We may be forgetful—sleep is often elusive—we may not eat properly—we may make foolish purchases—please don't condemn us. Just know it can be part of the grieving process. In time, we'll balance.

And please, oh please, let us follow our own timetables. We each march or stumble along the route at our own pace. Grief has no calendar. Don't hold us to a timetable.

For the moment, we are swimming—leaning literally on the love of God and our faith in Jesus Christ. This faith, along with your understanding, will help us eventually to celebrate life once again.